2025

The New Microsoft
Office 365
BIBLE

Achieve Mastery in Just 15 Minutes a Day! Illustrated Guide with Secret Tips and Shortcuts to Excel, Word, PowerPoint, and Impress Your Boss and Colleagues.

Word

Excel

Power Point

Access

5
Boost Productivity
BONUS

Outlook

Skype

Teams

One Drive

One Note

Publisher

10 IN 1

15
IN JUST 15
MINUTES/day

RICK STERLING

TABLE OF CONTETS

TABLE OF CONTENTS

Introduction

Can you imagine a computer without Word, Excel, or PowerPoint? If you were born after 1990, probably not. **Microsoft launched this suite for Windows in the early '90s**, revolutionizing office software. Initially installed using floppy disks (remember those?), then CD-ROMs, and finally via internet downloads with serial numbers, these programs have undergone numerous upgrades to become the powerful tools we use today.

Microsoft started with three core programs but quickly expanded its software offerings to cover various business needs. The suite has evolved from hardware-based to cloud-based, enabling **seamless online integration between tools**. This interconnectivity is a key feature of the Microsoft Suite, allowing for impressive cross-functionality. For instance, you can easily embed an Excel worksheet in a Word document or PowerPoint presentation, creating dynamic, data-driven documents.

The features and benefits of these programs have inspired similar software like Google Documents. If you compare the interfaces, you'll notice striking similarities. This is because the **Office Suite became the de facto standard in business software**, setting the benchmark for future applications. The **ribbon toolbar**, introduced in Office 2007, became the norm for these programs, offering an intuitive way to access features.

While this isn't a comprehensive history of Microsoft Office, its significance in the modern workplace can't be overstated. **Most jobs today require at least basic proficiency in these programs**. Many users can intuitively grasp basic functions, but a vast array of powerful features often remains undiscovered without further exploration. Don't worry – this

book will guide you through everything you need to know to become a pro user of these essential tools.

Did you know Excel boasts over 1,000 calculation functions, from simple sums to complex statistical analyses? Or that Word is far more than just a document writing program, offering advanced layout and collaboration features? Not to mention PowerPoint's ability to create dynamic, interactive presentations, or Access's power to build custom database applications. The Microsoft Suite opens up a world of possibilities for users at all levels, and with its continually enhanced features, it still dominates the market for both business and personal use.

Shortcut Features

A key factor in Microsoft Office's success was the implementation of keyboard shortcuts. Before Office, users had to input complex codes to format documents in programs like WordPerfect. Moreover, many computer users in the early days lacked a mouse – an expensive and relatively rare piece of hardware. Thus, the introduction of intuitive shortcuts was a game-changer, providing a faster alternative to mouse navigation and creating automated processes that attracted many users.

Are you aware that there are **over 100 keyboard shortcuts** available across these programs? On Windows PCs, you can access them by pressing the Ctrl key in combination with other keys. On MacOS, you use the Cmd or Command key instead. In both cases, the additional keys can be numbers, letters, or function keys like Shift or F5. These shortcuts can significantly speed up your workflow once mastered.

If you're unfamiliar with these shortcuts, don't worry. Each section of this book will provide a list of common shortcuts for specific programs, along with explanations of when and how to use them effectively. You'll also learn what makes each program unique – from basic features for everyday use to advanced functions for power users. Are you ready to start your journey to becoming a Microsoft Office pro? Let's dive in and unlock the full potential of these powerful tools!

Chapter 1:
Microsoft Word

Microsoft Word is the **cornerstone of document creation** in the modern digital age. From academic papers to business reports, and from creative writing to printable labels, Word's versatility is unmatched. While it's a staple for students crafting theses, its capabilities extend far beyond academic use. This powerhouse program offers a vast array of possibilities, seamlessly bridging professional and personal applications.

For businesses, Word excels in creating polished CVs, eye-catching brochures, and professional correspondence. On the personal front, it's equally adept at designing party invitations, crafting detailed itineraries, or even laying out a family newsletter. The software's flexibility allows it to adapt to virtually any text-based project you can imagine.

If you weren't fully aware of Word's extensive capabilities, don't worry. This comprehensive chapter will guide you through maximizing its potential, starting with the basics and progressing to advanced features that can transform your document creation process. Let's embark on this journey to Word mastery!

Navigating the Initial Interface

When you launch Microsoft Word, you're greeted with a welcoming interface designed for intuitive navigation. The opening window presents several options:

1. Open a new blank document (a clean slate for your ideas)
2. Choose from a variety of suggested templates (pre-formatted for specific purposes)
3. Access recently opened documents (for quick returns to works-in-progress)
4. View pinned documents (your frequently used files)

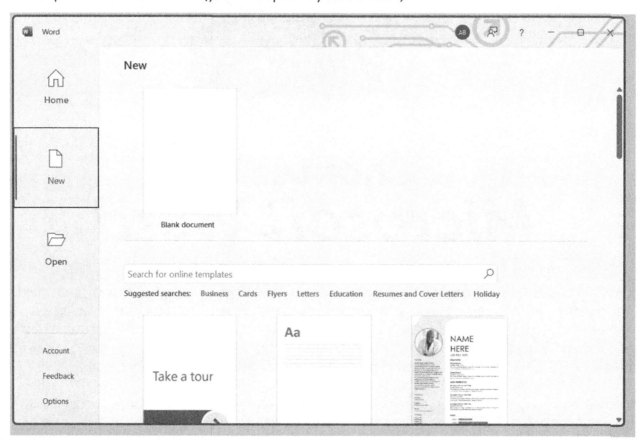

Pro tip: *Make the most of the pinning feature. By clicking the pin icon next to a document's last modification date, you ensure it remains easily accessible at the top of your list. This is particularly useful as your document collection grows, preventing important files from getting buried in the "recent" list.*

The left sidebar is your navigation hub, offering these essential options:

- **Home:** The initial screen, your starting point

- **New:** Create a blank document or choose from templates

- **Open:** Browse your computer or cloud storage for compatible files

- **Account:** View and manage your Microsoft account settings, check for software updates

- **Feedback:** Provide valuable input to help improve the program

- **Options:** Customize Word to suit your preferences and working style

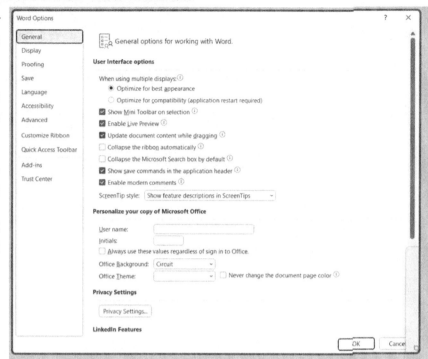

Options

Account

For this walkthrough, let's create a new document. Once selected, a pristine blank page appears, topped by the ribbon – Word's command center. Let's delve into the ribbon and unlock its powerful tools.

The Ribbon: Your Command Center

Let's explore the **key components of the Word ribbon**. This overview serves as an introduction, with each element detailed further in subsequent sections. Note that many functions have shortcuts, which we'll cover at the chapter's end for easy reference.

Upon opening a new document, you'll notice a **toolbar at the top**. If it's not visible, hover your cursor over the blue menu to reveal it. You can pin this ribbon for constant visibility by clicking the pin icon in the top-right corner. To hide it, click the arrow in the same location.

The **File tab** is your starting point, offering options to create, open, save, export, or print documents. We'll move on to other features since we've covered these basics.

Next is the **Home tab**, your formatting hub. It's divided into five sections: clipboard, font, paragraph, styles, and editing. The clipboard area allows you to paste, cut, copy, or use the format painter tool, which applies formatting from one text section to another.

The **font section** lets you customize your text's appearance. Choose fonts, make text bold, italic, or underlined, highlight text, and adjust color and size. The **paragraph feature** offers options for lists, indentation, text sorting, line spacing, and table design. The **style section** helps standardize titles and subtitles, useful for creating tables of contents. Lastly, the **editing area** enables you to find, replace, or select specific words or phrases.

MICROSOFT WORD

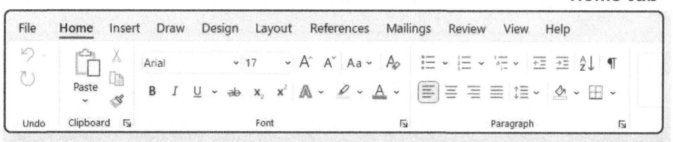

Ribbon

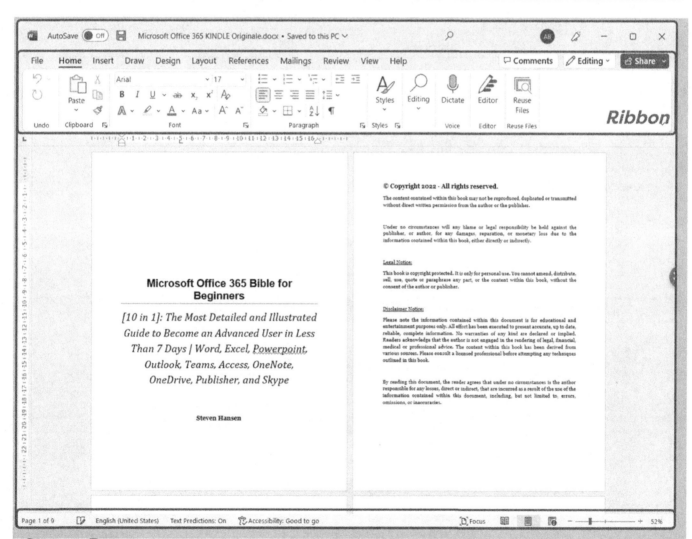

Microsoft Office 365 Bible for Beginners

[10 in 1]: The Most Detailed and Illustrated Guide to Become an Advanced User in Less Than 7 Days | Word, Excel, Powerpoint, Outlook, Teams, Access, OneNote, OneDrive, Publisher, and Skype

Steven Hansen

Status Bar

The **Insert tab** allows you to **add various elements** to your document, including headers, footers, images, and shapes. It's divided into ten sections: pages, tables, illustrations, add-ins, media, links, comments, header and footer, text, and symbols. You can add videos, edit links, and even input equations without manual calculations.

Insert tab

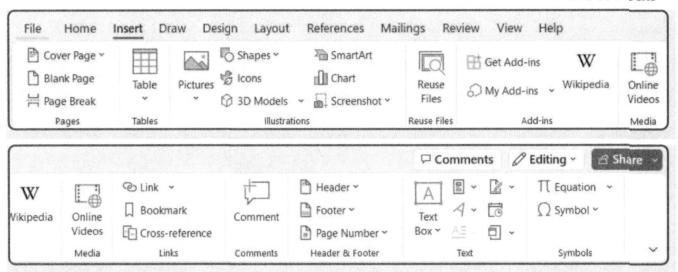

For example, to insert an image:

1. Click on the Insert tab.
2. Select **'Pictures'** from the Illustrations group.
3. Choose your image source (e.g., This Device, Stock Images, Online Pictures).
4. Select your image and click 'Insert'.

The **Design tab** offers **pre-set document designs** for quick formatting. This is especially helpful for creating professional-looking documents quickly. You can add background colors, borders, and watermarks, which is useful for drafts or controlled documents.

Design tab

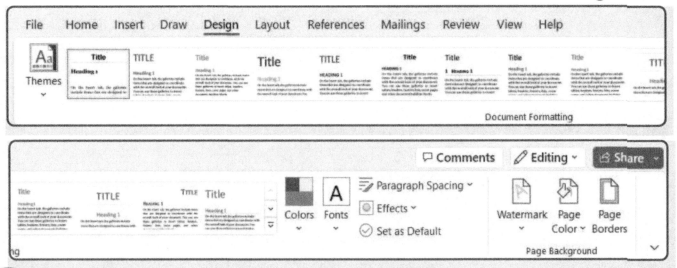

The **Layout tab** controls your document's structure. Set landscape or portrait orientation, divide text into columns, and fine-tune paragraph settings like indentation and line spacing. It also manages image alignment and text wrapping.

Layout tab

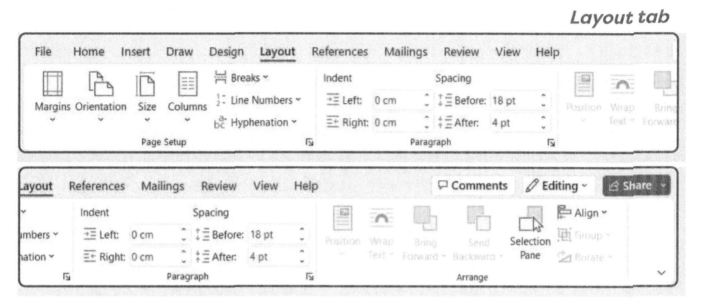

For books or theses, the **References tab** is invaluable. It includes tools for creating tables of contents, footnotes, citations, bibliographies, indexes, and more. It supports 12 citation styles, including APA and Harvard. This feature can save hours of manual formatting work.

References tab

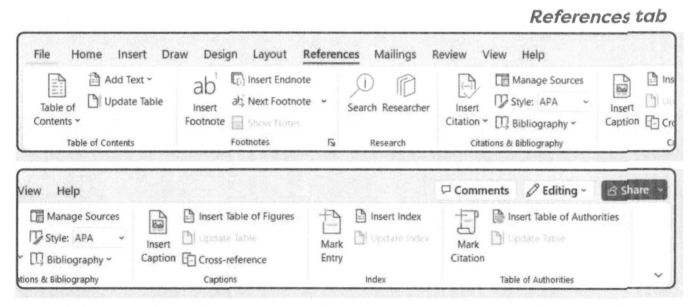

The **Mailing tab** is perfect for **business applications**, helping create mailing lists and labels. Imagine easily printing address labels for Christmas cards! The mail merge feature allows you to personalize mass mailings efficiently.

Mailings tab

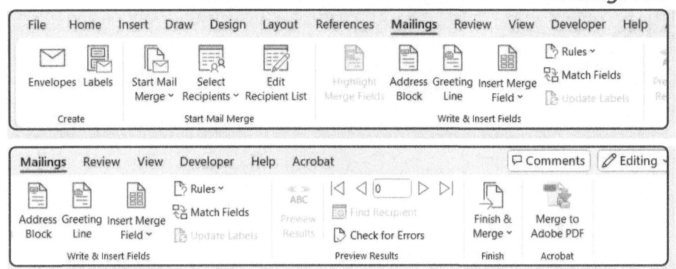

After completing your document, use the **Review tab** for editing and proofreading. It offers tools for tracking changes, adding comments, translating text, and comparing document versions. This is crucial for collaborative work and maintaining document integrity.

Review tab

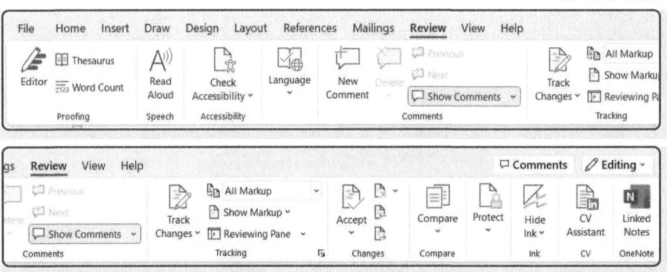

The **View tab** lets you customize how you see your document on screen. Adjust zoom levels, show/hide rulers, split the window, and more. This flexibility can greatly enhance your productivity.

View tab

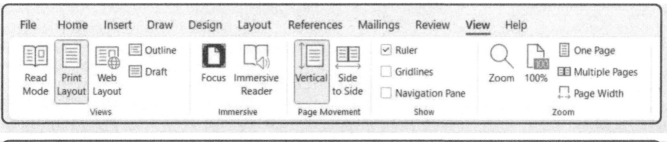

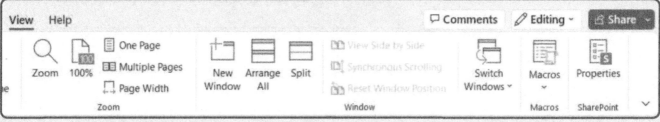

Lastly, the **Help button** provides support, feedback options, and answers to your questions about Word's features. Don't hesitate to use this resource if you're stuck or want to learn more about a specific feature..

Help tab

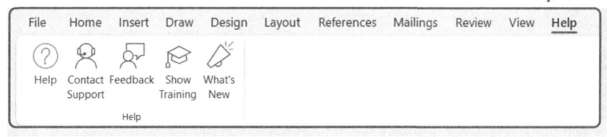

Remember the **thin gray line at the bottom** of your document? It's the status bar, providing essential document information. Let's explore its significance next. By mastering these ribbon features, you'll be well on your way to becoming a Word power user, capable of creating sophisticated documents with ease.

The Status Bar: Your Document's Information Hub

The status bar, located at the bottom of your Word window, provides **crucial document information at a glance**. First, you'll see the page count, displayed as "**page x of x**". This quick reference helps you gauge your document's length and current position.

Next, the **word count** feature offers more than just a total tally. When you select a portion of text, it dynamically updates to show "**x of x words**", indicating the selected word count relative to the total. This functionality is particularly useful for writers working within specific word limits, as it provides immediate feedback on section lengths.

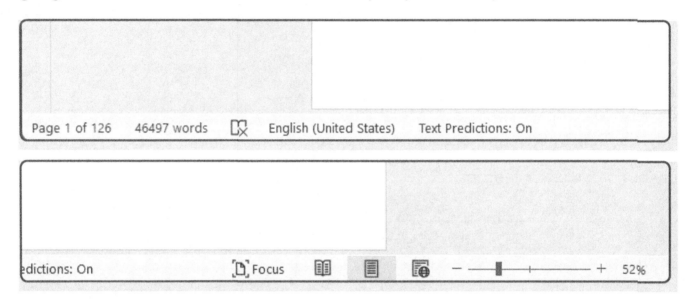
The small book icon serves as a **proofreading indicator**. A checkmark signifies no errors, while an 'x' indicates necessary corrections. Double-clicking this icon opens the proofreading pane, allowing you to address issues efficiently. This feature utilizes complex natural language processing algorithms to identify grammatical and spelling errors contextually.

Adjacent to the proofreading icon is the **language indicator**, showing the current proofing language with its country variant (e.g., English (United States)). This specificity is crucial as it accounts for regional linguistic variations, ensuring accurate proofreading. To change the language, double-click this indicator and select your preferred option from the menu.

Page 1 of 126   46497 words   English (United States)   Text Predictions: On

edictions: On   Focus   52%

Initiating Your Word Journey

To start a new document in Word, click the **File** button and select **New Document**. This action triggers the creation of a blank canvas, initializing a new instance of the Word document object model in the background.

The **Save** and **Save As** functions, also found under the File menu, utilize different processes. **"Save"** updates the existing file, while **"Save As"** creates a new file instance, allowing you to change the name, location, or file format (e.g., .pdf). This distinction is crucial for version control and file management.

To open an existing document, navigate to the File tab. Here, you'll find a list of recent documents and pinned files, leveraging Word's file caching system for quick access. Alternatively, click **Open** on the left toolbar to browse your computer's file system.

Word's **template feature** offers pre-designed document structures. These templates are XML-based files that define document formatting, styles, and content placeholders. Utilizing templates can significantly reduce document setup time and ensure consistency across similar document types.

? — ☐ ✕

Leveraging Templates in Word

Word intelligently identifies your frequently used documents, suggesting them on the home page. For more options, click **"More templates"** to access a comprehensive catalog categorized by document type. From resumes to party invitations, the variety is extensive. The search bar allows you to explore online templates, expanding your options beyond the local database. This feature utilizes machine learning algorithms to predict user preferences and offer relevant suggestions.

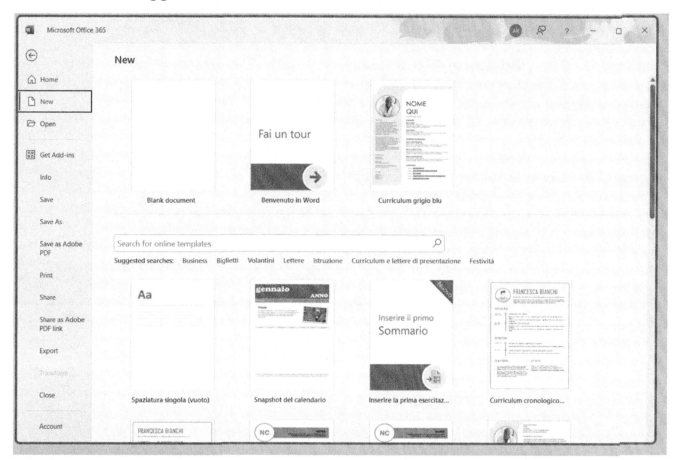

Text Formatting: The Art of Document Presentation

The visual presentation of a document, from font color to text alignment, can significantly impact its effectiveness. This section will guide you through the intricacies of text formatting to optimize your document's appearance.

Word Processing Fundamentals

When initiating a new document, defining font type, size, and color is crucial.

The **Home tab's font section** offers two approaches: format as you type or apply changes post-writing. The font dialog box, accessible via the arrow next to **"Font,"** provides a preview of your selections, employing real-time rendering techniques to display changes instantly.

This dialog box offers standard options like font style, size, and color, as well as advanced features such as superscript and strikethrough. The **"Advanced" tab** allows for precise character spacing and positioning adjustments, utilizing sophisticated typographic algorithms to enhance readability and aesthetic appeal.

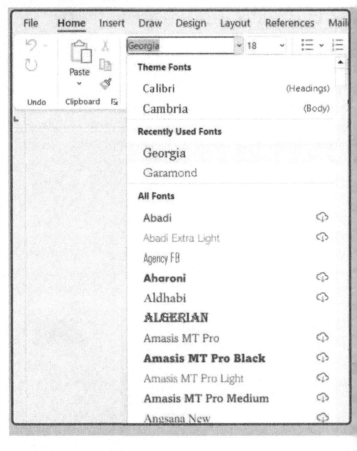

The ribbon interface provides quick access to common formatting options. The font dropdown menu visually displays each typeface, leveraging vector graphics for crisp rendering at any size. Font size can be adjusted via the dropdown or by typing a specific value, offering granular control over text dimensions.

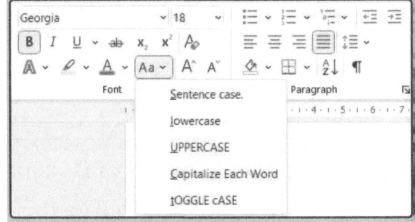

The case change button **(Aa)** alters text capitalization without retyping, using string manipulation algorithms to efficiently transform selected text. Other easily accessible functions include highlighting, font color, superscript, subscript, and strikethrough.

A notable feature is the **"Clear Formatting" button ("A" with a pink square)**, which resets text to default settings. This function uses cascading style sheet (CSS) principles to efficiently remove applied formatting, offering a faster alternative to multiple undo operations.

> **Pro tip:** In the **home tab** of the ribbon, you'll spot a paintbrush icon. This tool, known as the **Format Painter**, efficiently replicates formatting across your document.

? — □ ✕

Here's how to utilize this powerful feature:

1. Select the text with the desired formatting.
2. Click the paintbrush icon once for single use, or **twice** for multiple applications.
3. Highlight the text you want to format.
4. The selected text instantly adopts the copied style.

This tool leverages **style inheritance principles**, temporarily storing a complex set of formatting attributes in memory. When applied, it uses **cascading style application algorithms** to ensure all properties are correctly transferred and rendered.

The Format Painter's efficiency lies in its ability to copy and apply multiple formatting properties simultaneously, including font characteristics, paragraph settings, and even advanced features like styles and themes. This is achieved through a sophisticated **attribute mapping system** that ensures accurate replication across different text segments.

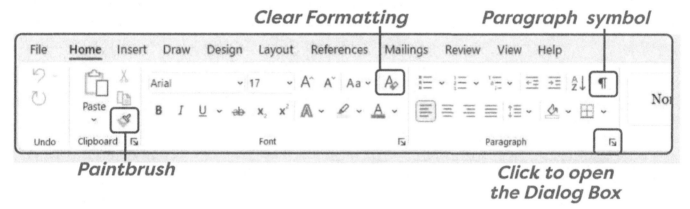

Clear Formatting   *Paragraph symbol*

Paintbrush   *Click to open the Dialog Box*

Paragraph formatting

After tailoring your text's appearance, the next step is **paragraph formatting**. While Word defaults to left alignment, this can be easily modified. The **paragraph function**, like its font counterpart, features a dropdown menu leading to a comprehensive dialogue box. This interface, while less intuitive than ribbon buttons, offers advanced tools and a real-time preview of your selections.

*Pro tip: The **paragraph symbol** button (¶) in the top-right corner of the paragraph section is a powerful formatting aid. It reveals non-printing characters, including spaces, paragraph breaks, and tabs. This feature, which employs Unicode characters for visualization, doesn't affect the final output but proves invaluable for precise formatting.*

For instance, when composing a letter, you might want the address in the top-right corner. Simply select the **right** alignment button.

For centered titles, use the **centered** option, and for text justified on both margins, apply the **justified** setting. These options, represented by intuitive icons on the ribbon, utilize sophisticated text flow algorithms to distribute text optimally.

The **indentation** feature allows you to offset the first line of each paragraph, while line spacing controls vertical text distribution.

The line spacing dropdown (represented by up and down arrows) offers preset options like 1.0, 1.5, or 2.0, which use percentage-based calculations to adjust inter-line gaps. For more granular control, the **line spacing options** allow custom settings, including space before or after paragraphs.

This level of control is particularly crucial for academic or scientific writing, where precise formatting is often mandatory.

The **set as default** button applies your chosen settings globally, either to the current document or all future documents based on the normal template.

This feature leverages Word's template system, which stores formatting as XML-based style definitions for consistent application.

The paragraph section also facilitates **list creation**, offering **bullet points** and **numbered lists.** These features employ hierarchical data structures to maintain order and indentation. The multilevel list option uses a tree-like structure for complex nested lists.

Organize a list in alphabetical order

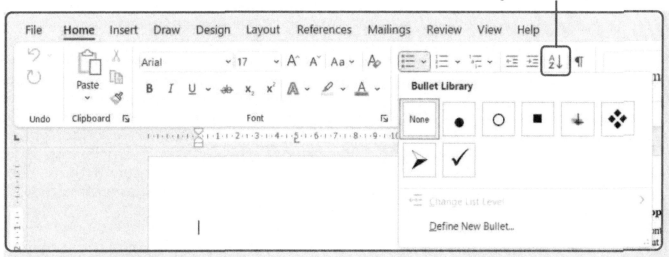

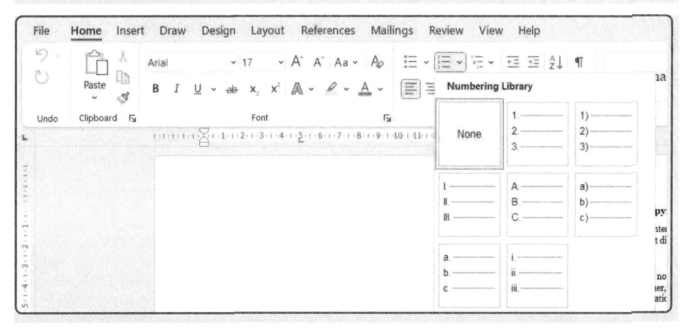

Pro tip: *Word's list function uses pattern recognition algorithms for automatic continuation. Pressing* **Enter** *creates a new list item, while* **Tab** *initiates a sub-level, triggering the list's internal hierarchy adjustment. This intelligent system streamlines the creation of structured content, enhancing both efficiency and document organization.*

Continuing with paragraph formatting, Word offers additional powerful features to enhance document organization and visual appeal. The alphabetical sorting option, represented by the **'AZ↓' button,** employs a sophisticated **quicksort algorithm** to efficiently reorder list items. This feature is particularly useful for organizing references, glossaries, or any list that benefits from alphabetical arrangement.

The **square button** in the ribbon activates the border function, which utilizes vector graphics rendering for crisp, scalable formatting. This tool allows you to frame text or add lines to specific sides of a paragraph, enhancing visual hierarchy and document structure. The border feature uses a grid-based system to accurately position lines relative to the text.

For adding color, the **paint bucket** tool implements a flood fill algorithm to apply color to paragraphs, sections, or lines. This feature interacts with Word's layered document structure, ensuring that color is applied correctly to the desired elements without affecting surrounding content.

An advanced layout feature in Word is the ability to create multi-column text, ideal for newspaper-style articles or brochures. To access this, navigate to the **layout** tab and select the **columns** button. This feature employs sophisticated **text flow algorithms** to distribute content across multiple columns dynamically.

Layout tab

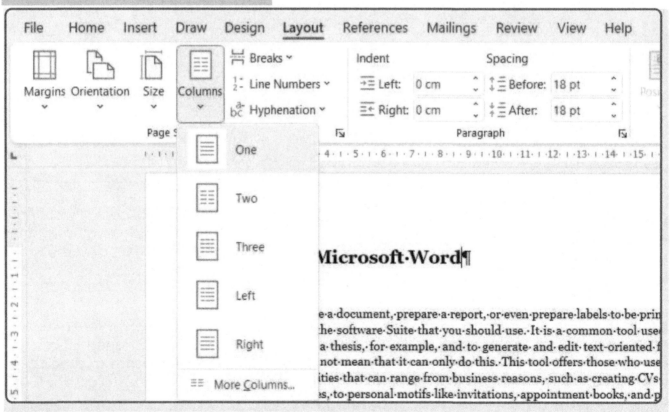

The basic column settings allow you to specify the number of columns, while the advanced dialogue box offers more granular control. Here, you can:

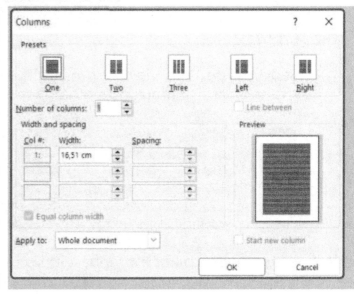

1. Adjust column width using precise measurements

2. Set the spacing between columns (known as "gutter" in typography)

3. Add vertical lines between columns for visual separation

4. Define where the column layout should be applied within the document

Formatting and Viewing the Document: Optimizing Visual Presentation

After perfecting your text's format, the next crucial step is fine-tuning the overall document layout. Microsoft Word offers a robust suite of features designed to give you precise control over your document's appearance. To gain the most comprehensive view of your document's formatting and layout, navigate to the **View tab** in the ribbon and select **Print layout view**. This viewing mode utilizes a **WYSIWYG (What you see is what you get)** rendering engine, providing a highly accurate representation of how your document will appear when printed or saved as a PDF.

View tab

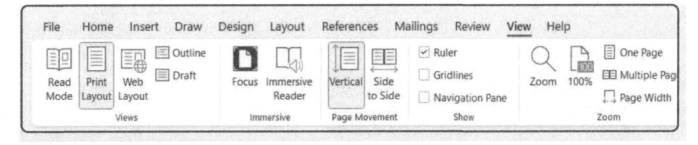

1. **Print layout View:** employs sophisticated rendering algorithms that balance visual fidelity with performance. This view accurately displays:

- Margins and page boundaries
- Headers and footers
- Multi-column layouts
- Floating images with text wrapping

In addition to print layout view, Word offers other viewing options, each designed for specific purposes:

2. **Read mode:** This view optimizes the document for on-screen reading. It employs screen space optimization algorithms to maximize the content area, hiding toolbars and adjusting the layout for easier consumption on various devices. This mode often uses a pageless layout and adjusts text size and column width for optimal readability.

3. **Draft view:** This simplified view focuses on content rather than layout. It omits certain visual elements like page margins and some graphics to improve performance. Draft view uses a streamlined rendering engine that prioritizes text display and basic formatting, making it ideal for rapid content creation and editing.

Each view employs different rendering techniques:

- **Print Layout:** High-fidelity visual representation
- **Read Mode:** Adaptive layout for readability
- **Draft View:** Simplified rendering for speed

Configuring Page Layout and Margins

Begin by setting your page **orientation** to either **landscape** or **portrait**. Navigate to the **layout** tab and select your preference from the **orientation** dropdown. This fundamental change instantly alters your document's visual structure.

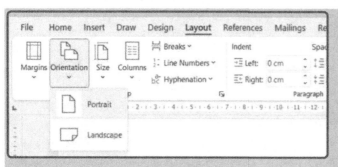

Next, customize your margins. In the same ribbon area, click **margins** to choose from preset options or create custom settings. The **customize margins** dialog box allows precise control over margin dimensions.

? — □ ✕

Pro tip: *For visual margin adjustment, utilize the* **ruler** *feature. Toggle it on/off in the* **view** *tab. The ruler displays non-printing guidelines, allowing you to manipulate margins and paragraph indentations using the double arrows. This feature employs a real-time coordinate system to update document layout dynamically.*

Ruler

The margin dialog box also offers advanced options like **book fold** settings and **paper size** selection. The **paper** tab allows standard or custom paper dimensions. These settings leverage sophisticated page layout algorithms to ensure consistent document formatting across various output media.

To start a new section on a fresh page, use the **page break** feature instead of multiple line returns. Access this in the **insert** tab under **pages**, along with options for **cover pages** and **blank pages**. Page breaks utilize document object model manipulation to create logical document divisions.

Insert tab

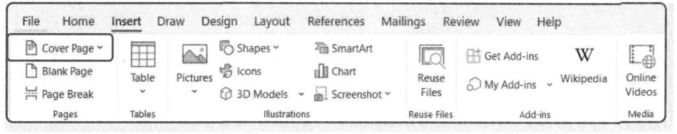

Cover Pages options

For more nuanced breaks, the **layout** tab offers options like column breaks and text wrapping breaks. **Section breaks** provide even more control, allowing you to start new sections on the next page, continue on the same page, or begin on even/odd pages. These features employ complex layout management algorithms to maintain document structure integrity.

Understanding these foundational tools sets the stage for exploring Word's more advanced features. Next, we'll delve into enhancing your document with additional functions, starting with table management.

Layout tab

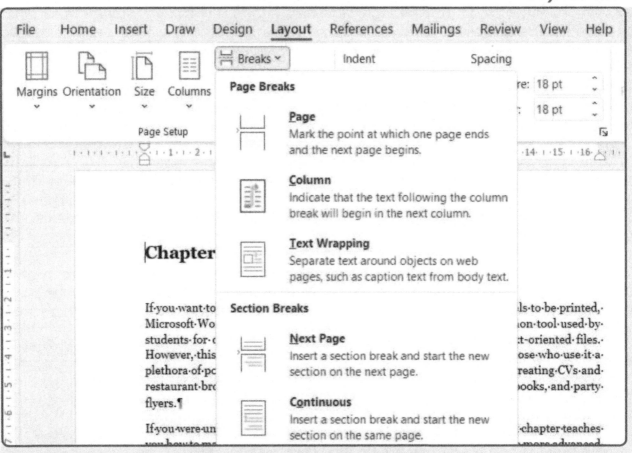

Enhancing Document Structure with Tables

Tables serve as powerful tools for organizing content in documents. Microsoft Word offers a user-friendly interface for table creation and manipulation, leveraging sophisticated data structure algorithms to maintain document integrity.

To insert a table, navigate to the **insert** tab and locate the **table** section. The dropdown menu utilizes a dynamic grid system, allowing you to visually select your desired table dimensions. As you hover over the grid, real-time preview algorithms update the display, showing your potential table configuration.

For precise control, the **insert table** dialog offers manual input for rows and columns. This interface interacts with Word's document object model, ensuring that table dimensions are accurately reflected in the underlying XML structure. A noteworthy feature is the ability to **draw** tables freehand or insert an **Excel spreadsheet**. The latter employs inter-application communication protocols, seamlessly integrating Excel's computational power within your Word document. This feature utilizes COM (Component Object Model) technology to maintain live links between the two applications, ensuring data consistency.

> **Pro tip:** *Upon table insertion, Word dynamically generates a context-sensitive **table tools** tab. This adaptive user interface employs state-based logic to present relevant options based on your current table selection.*

Table Design Tab include this Key features:

1. **Design customization:** Utilizes vector graphics rendering for table styles and borders.

2. **Layout manipulation:** Employs grid-based algorithms for row/column management.

3. **Cell operations:** Uses matrix manipulation techniques for merging, splitting, and resizing cells.

4. **Data sorting:** Implements efficient sorting algorithms for organizing table content.

These tools interact with Word's text formatting engine, allowing consistent styling across table and non-table content. The table functionality in Word demonstrates the software's

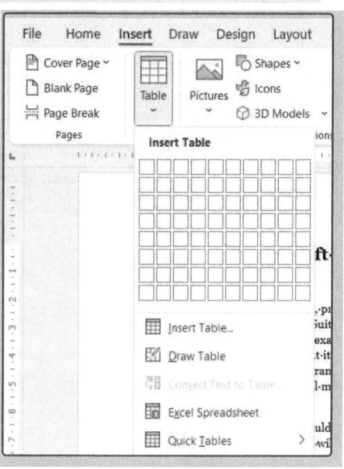

ability to handle complex data structures within a rich text environment, balancing user accessibility with powerful backend processing. Understanding these table features opens up new possibilities for data presentation and organization within your documents, enhancing both clarity and analytical capabilities.

Create Graphs and Formulas

For business reports requiring statistical representation, Word offers robust **data visualization tools**. Navigate to the **insert** tab and locate the **illustrations** section to access the chart feature. This functionality leverages advanced graphing algorithms to transform raw data into meaningful visual representations.

Insert tab

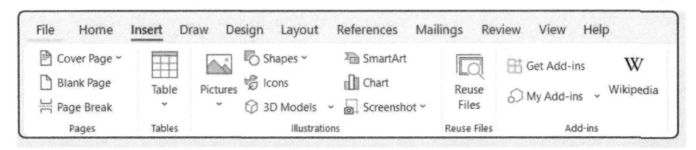

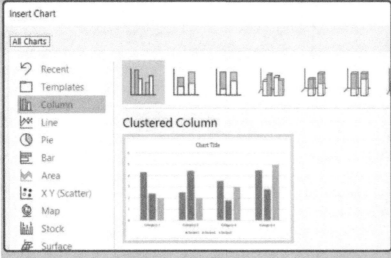

Upon selecting the chart option, a dialog box presents various chart types, from basic column charts to complex histograms. This selection process utilizes a dynamic rendering engine to provide real-time previews of each chart type.

Once you choose a chart, Word generates a placeholder image alongside an embedded **Excel spreadsheet**.

This integration demonstrates Word's interoperability with Excel, using COM (Component Object Model) technology for seamless data exchange. The spreadsheet is pre-formatted with labeled cells, employing intelligent data mapping to streamline the input process.

> **Pro tip:** *To modify the underlying data, use the **Edit Data** option. For external data sources, the **Select Data** function allows you to import data from other files. This feature utilizes advanced file I/O operations and data parsing algorithms to integrate external information seamlessly.*

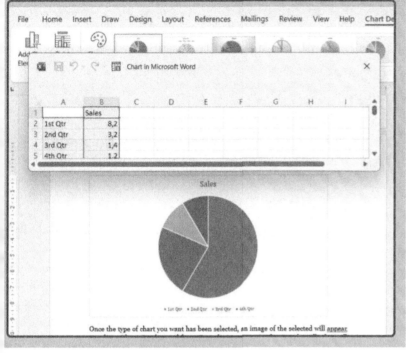

The **Chart tools** contextual tab appears when working with charts, offering additional customization options. This adaptive interface employs state-based logic to present relevant tools based on the selected chart type. Key features include:

1. **Chart elements:** Utilizes modular chart components for easy addition or removal.

2. **Layout options:** Employs layout algorithms to optimize chart presentation.

3. **Style presets:** Uses pre-defined style templates for quick visual enhancements.

4. **Color schemes:** Implements color theory algorithms for harmonious palettes.

The **Format** tab within **Chart tools** provides granular control over individual chart elements, leveraging vector graphics manipulation for precise adjustments.

Chart Design tab

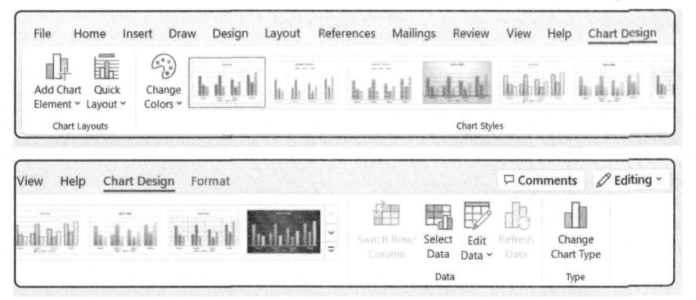

Chart resizing can be done manually or by inputting specific dimensions. The manual method uses real-time scaling algorithms, while dimensional input employs precise pixel-based rendering.

For text integration, the **wrap text** function in the **arrange** tab offers various text wrapping options. This feature uses advanced layout algorithms to dynamically adjust text flow around the chart, maintaining document readability and visual appeal.

Pictures, Shapes, and SmartArt

These **visual enhancement tools** in Microsoft Word offer powerful ways to augment your documents. Each category, while distinct, shares commonalities in functionality and purpose. Let's explore them in detail:

Pictures

To insert images, use the **insert tab** or keyboard shortcuts. Word supports both local and online image sources, leveraging advanced file I/O and network protocols for seamless integration.

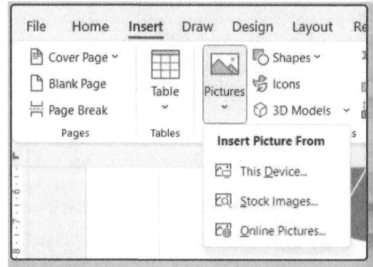

Upon insertion, a **context-sensitive toolbar** appears, offering image manipulation options.

The **corrections button** in the adjust section utilizes sophisticated image processing algorithms for enhancing picture quality. The ability to reset changes demonstrates Word's implementation of non-destructive editing techniques.

Picture Format tab

Pro tip: The **compress image** feature employs lossy and lossless compression algorithms to reduce file size while maintaining visual quality. This function is crucial for optimizing document performance and storage efficiency.

Manual adjustment of pictures involves real-time scaling and positioning algorithms. The **crop** feature uses vector-based clipping paths for precise image trimming.

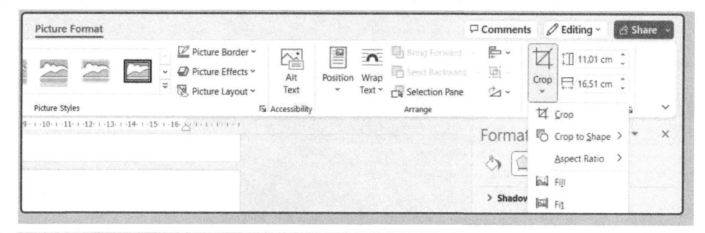

Pro tip: Holding the shift key while resizing maintains aspect ratio through proportional scaling algorithms, preventing image distortion.

Shapes

Shape insertion, similar to pictures, is accessed via the **insert tab**. Word offers a variety of pre-defined vector shapes, categorized for easy selection. These shapes are rendered using scalable vector graphics (SVG) technology, ensuring crisp appearance at any size.

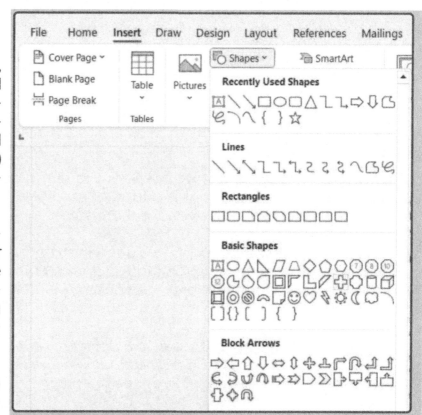

The **shape format tab** provides extensive customization options. Color fill and border adjustments utilize advanced color management systems. Shape manipulation, including rotation, employs affine transformation matrices for precise control.

Text can be added to shapes, with Word's text flow algorithms auto-

matically adjusting to the shape's boundaries. The **text wrap** feature uses complex layout algorithms to integrate shapes seamlessly with surrounding text.

Shape Format tab

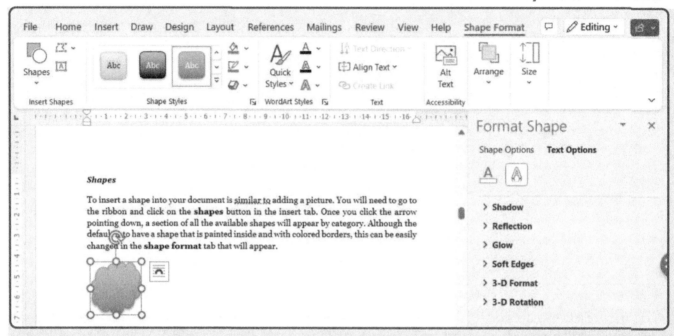

Pro tip: *Yellow control points on shapes activate parametric shape modification, allowing fine-tuned adjustments without altering the overall shape integrity.*

SmartArt

SmartArt represents Word's implementation of **data visualization for conceptual information**. Accessed through the **insert tab**, it offers pre-designed layouts for processes, hierarchies, and cycles.

The SmartArt feature employs intelligent layout algorithms that automatically adjust the graphic's structure as content is added or modified. This dynamic resizing ensures optimal use of space and maintains visual coherence.

A dedicated **SmartArt tab** appears upon insertion, offering tools for structure modification and style adjustment. These tools interact with Word's general formatting engine, allowing consistent styling across different document elements.

Pro tip: *The add shape function in SmartArt uses context-aware insertion algorithms. By selecting a specific element before adding a shape, you can precisely control the new element's position within the structure's hierarchy.*

SmartArtDesign tab

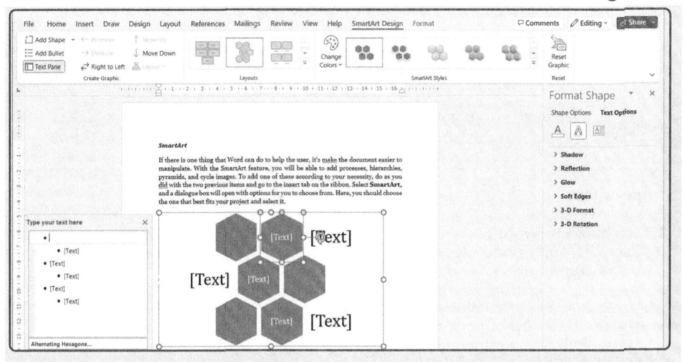

These visual tools demonstrate Word's sophisticated integration of various graphical technologies, from bitmap manipulation to vector graphics and data-driven visualizations, all within a user-friendly interface.

Creating a Table of Contents, Footnotes, Captions and Bibliography

Microsoft Word's **automated document structuring features** significantly streamline the process of creating professional, well-organized documents. These tools leverage advanced algorithms to generate tables of contents and manage references with minimal manual input. Let's explore these powerful features in detail.

Table of Contents

Creating a table of contents in Word is a **semi-automated process** that relies on the strategic use of the **Styles** feature in the **Home tab.** This system employs a hierarchical structure to organize document content:

- **Heading 1**: Typically used for chapter titles
- **Heading 2**: For main section subtitles
- **Heading 3** and beyond: For progressively nested subsections

This hierarchical approach utilizes a tree-like data structure in the background, allowing Word to efficiently organize and later retrieve document structure information.

Home tab

To apply styles:

1. Select the relevant text
2. Click the appropriate heading style in the Styles gallery

Word uses visual cues (small squares and arrows) to indicate style application, employing user interface design principles to enhance usability.

> *Pro tip:* Style customization is achieved through context menus or direct modification. The **"Update Heading x to match selection"** feature uses pattern matching algorithms to propagate style changes across the document, ensuring consistency.

To generate the table of contents:

1. Navigate to the **reference** tab
2. Click the **Table of Contents** button
3. Select your preferred style

This process triggers Word's document analysis algorithms, which scan the document for styled headings and compile them into a structured table. The table of contents is a dynamic element, capable of being updated to reflect document changes.

The update feature uses diff algorithms to identify changes in the document structure and efficiently refreshes the table of contents without regenerating it entirely. These automated features demonstrate Word's sophisticated document management capabilities, combining ease of use with powerful backend processing to handle complex document structures.

References tab

Inserting Footnotes

Footnotes are crucial for **academic and professional documents**. Word's footnote feature employs an intelligent numbering system and dynamic page layout algorithms.

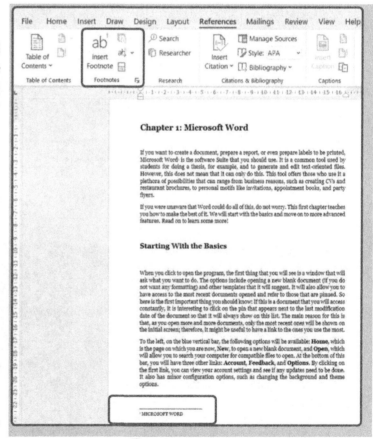

Footnote

To insert a footnote:

1. Position the cursor next to the relevant word

2. Navigate to the **reference** tab

3. Click **Insert Footnote**

This action triggers several processes:

- A superscript number is inserted in the main text

- The cursor is automatically moved to the page footer

- A corresponding footnote marker is created

Word uses a **linked text flow algorithm** to maintain the connection between the reference and the footnote. This system allows for automatic renumbering and repositioning of footnotes as the document is edited.

The **Next footnote** button utilizes document navigation algorithms to quickly traverse through footnotes, enhancing editing efficiency.

Inserting Captions

Caption insertion is integral for **document organization and referencing**. To add a caption:

1. Select the target image or object
2. Click **Insert caption** in the reference tab

This opens a dialog box where you can:

- Name the caption
- Categorize it (figure, equation, table)
- Set numbering preferences

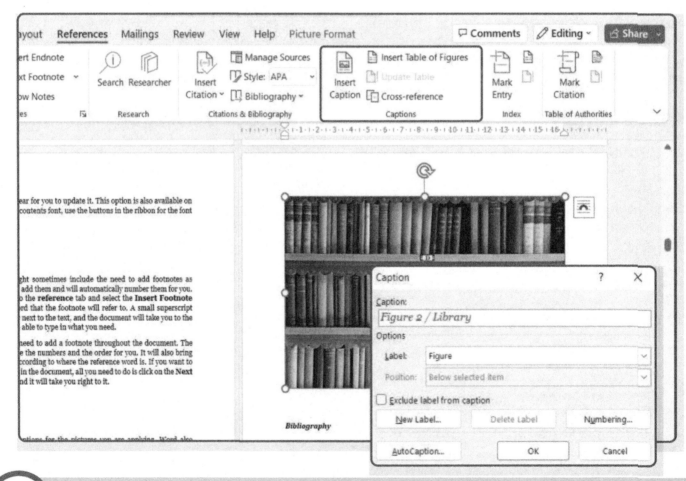

Word employs a **dynamic labeling system** that can incorporate chapter numbers or use simple sequential numbering. This system interfaces with the document's structural metadata to ensure consistent and accurate captioning.

The ability to generate a table of figures leverages the same algorithms used for the table of contents, creating a navigable index of visual elements in the document.

Bibliography

Word's bibliography feature is a powerful tool for **academic writing and citation management**. The process involves:

1. Selecting a **citation style** (e.g., APA, Vancouver, ISO)

2. Using the **Insert Citation** button to input source information

3. Generating the bibliography with the **Bibliography** button

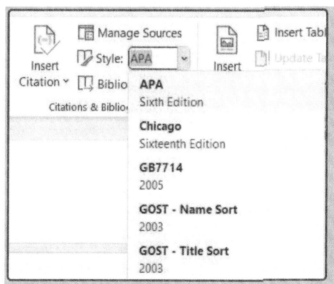

This system utilizes a **structured data approach**, storing citation information in a standardized format. When generating the bibliography, Word applies style-specific formatting rules to each entry, ensuring consistency and accuracy.

The bibliography feature demonstrates Word's capability to handle complex, rule-based text formatting tasks, significantly reducing the cognitive load on the user for citation management.

These advanced features showcase Word's sophisticated document management capabilities, combining user-friendly interfaces with powerful backend processing to handle complex academic and professional writing tasks efficiently.

Spell Check and Language Tools

Spell check is a **critical feature for document credibility**. Word's spell check functionality employs sophisticated natural language processing (NLP) algorithms to detect and suggest corrections for spelling and grammatical errors.

To set the language for spell check:

1. Click the language in the **status bar**
2. Or access the **review** tab on the ribbon

Review tab

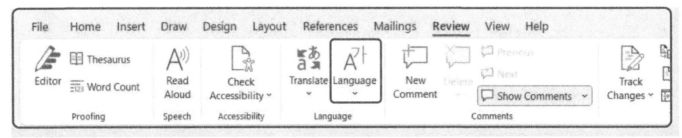

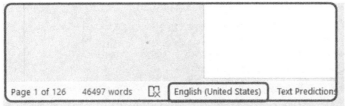

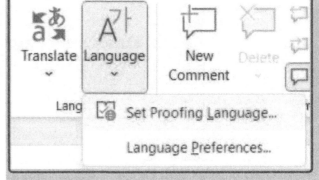

Word's language detection algorithms allow for:

- Whole document proofreading
- Section-specific language checks

The translation feature leverages **machine learning-based translation models**. Options include:

- Full document translation
- Selected section translation
- Hover-over mini translations

This system integrates with online language models, continuously updating to improve accuracy. Post-translation spell checking ensures linguistic coherence and correctness.

Document Review and Collaboration

For collaborative editing, Word offers powerful **track changes** functionality:

1. Activate the **Tracking** function
2. Edit the document
3. Changes are visually marked and logged

Review tab

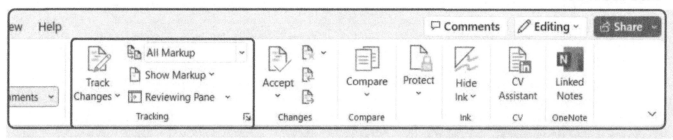

This feature utilizes a sophisticated **diff algorithm** to identify and highlight modifications. Reviewers can then:

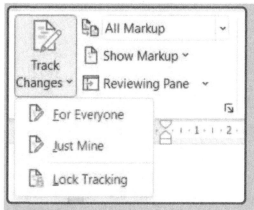

- Accept changes individually or en masse
- Reject suggestions as needed

The **Compare** function is particularly useful when changes haven't been tracked. It employs advanced **document comparison algorithms** to:

- Analyze the original and modified versions
- Identify differences at character, word, and structural levels
- Present a comprehensive view of all alterations

This system allows for efficient review of edits, even when collaborators haven't used the built-in tracking features.

These advanced editing and collaboration tools demonstrate Word's capability to handle complex document workflows. By integrating NLP for spell checking, machine translation for language conversion, and sophisticated diff algorithms for change tracking, Word provides a comprehensive suite for document refinement and collaborative work. These features not only enhance document quality but also streamline the review process, making it an indispensable tool for professional and academic writing.

Keyboard Shortcuts on Word

FUNCTION	PC SHORTCUT	MAC SHORTCUT
Start a new document	Ctrl + N	Command + N
Open a new document	Ctrl + O	Command + O
Save the document	Ctrl + S	Command + S
Cut content	Ctrl + X	Command + X or F2
Paste content	Ctrl + V	Command + V or F4
Copy content	Ctrl + C	Command + C or F3
Make font bold	Ctrl + B	Command + B
Underline selection	Ctrl + U	Command + U
Make font italic	Ctrl + I	Command + I
Undo previous action	Ctrl + Z	Command + Z or F1
Print	Ctrl + P	Command + P
Move cursor to top	Ctrl + Alt + Page Up	Command + Page Up
Move cursor down	Ctrl + Alt + Page Down	Command + Page Down
Select whole document	Ctrl + A	Command + A
Insert page break	Ctrl + Enter	Command + Return
Insert line break	Shift + Enter	Shift + Return
Insert column break	Ctrl + Shift + Enter	Command + Shift + Return
Insert copyright symbol	Ctrl + Alt + C	Not available
Insert trademark symbol	Ctrl + Alt + T	Option + 2

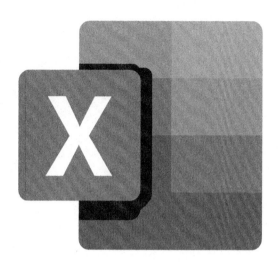

Chapter 2:
Microsoft Excel

A Versatile Computational Tool

Excel, part of the Microsoft Office Suite, is primarily used for **data analysis, financial management, and complex calculations**. However, its capabilities extend far beyond basic arithmetic. Excel allows users to **create forms, generate graphs, and perform in-depth data analysis**. Some advanced users even leverage Excel's power to develop simple programs.

Before delving into Excel's specifics, it's worth noting that many features of the Office ribbon interface are consistent across applications. This chapter will focus on Excel-specific tools and functions.

Fundamentals

When launching Excel for the first time, you'll encounter a **grid-based document** known as a **spreadsheet**, which forms the foundation of this powerful data analysis tool. By default, Excel opens a single **worksheet**, representing your primary project area. For complex projects requiring multiple related datasets, you can create additional worksheets by clicking

the '+' icon adjacent to the sheet tabs. This feature leverages Excel's **relational data model**, allowing for interconnected data across numerous sheets.

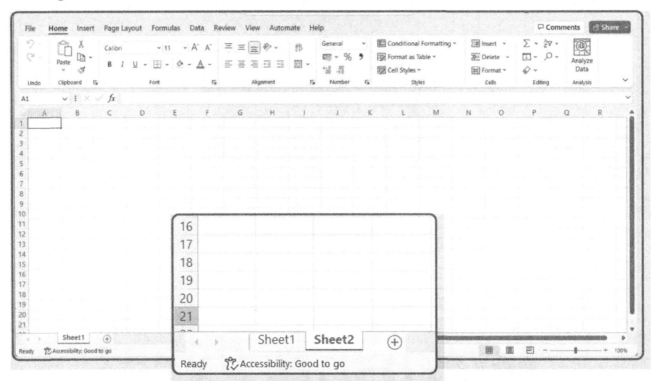

Pro tip: *Enhance your worksheet management by* **customizing sheet names and tab colors**. *To rename a worksheet, simply double-click its default name (e.g., "Sheet1") and input your desired title. For visual organization, right-click the tab and select* **Tab Color**. *This context menu also offers options to move, protect, or hide sheets. Exercise caution when deleting sheets, as this action is* **irreversible** *and can lead to critical data loss.*

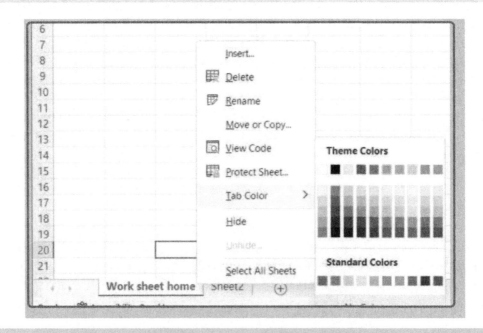

Excel's interface utilizes a **Cartesian coordinate system**, with columns designated by letters and rows by numbers. This **alphanumeric grid** is crucial for cell referencing in formulas, which we'll explore in depth later.

To adjust column or row dimensions, position your cursor on the dividing line until a double arrow appears, then drag to resize. This **dynamic resizing** feature allows for precise control over data presentation.

> **Pro tip:** *Excel incorporates an **intelligent content-aware sizing algorithm**. To automatically adjust a column's width to accommodate its contents, double-click the column divider. This **auto-fit function** analyzes the longest content in the column and optimizes the width accordingly, saving time and ensuring data visibility.*

While Excel shares many formatting tools with Word, it boasts unique features tailored for **data manipulation and analysis**. These capabilities harness **advanced statistical methods** and **machine learning algorithms** to extract insights from complex datasets. For instance, Excel's **PivotTable feature** employs sophisticated data aggregation techniques to summarize large datasets dynamically.

Excel's cell-based structure enables efficient **data organization and processing**. Each cell functions as a discrete unit capable of storing various data types, including numbers, text, dates, and formulas. This flexibility, combined with Excel's **powerful calculation engine**, allows users to create intricate models and perform real-time data analysis.

The software's **formula language** is a robust scripting system rooted in **fundamental computer science principles**. It supports everything from basic arithmetic to complex financial modeling, enabling users to create sophisticated logical structures within their spreadsheets. For example, Excel's **IF function** implements conditional branching, a core concept in programming, allowing for dynamic data evaluation and decision-making within cells.

Layout and Visualization Tools

Excel's **layout and visualization features** enhance spreadsheet functionality and reveal hidden capabilities. The software offers three viewing modes, accessible from the bottom-right corner: **Normal**, **Page Layout**, and **Page Break Preview**. Let's explore the latter two, as they provide unique insights beyond the standard working view.

Page Layout View

This mode combines editing functionality with header and footer visibility, crucial for .pdf exports or printed documents.

The **Page Layout** tab enables toggling between **portrait and landscape orientations**, visualizing **page breaks**, and adjusting **margins**. These features utilize Excel's **advanced document rendering engine**, which dynamically adjusts the spreadsheet's visual representation based on selected parameters.

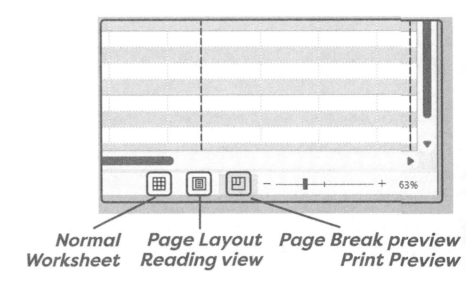

Normal Worksheet   *Page Layout Reading view*   *Page Break preview Print Preview*

Header and Footer Customization: Excel's headers and footers are divided into three sections, maintaining consistency regardless of column count. This **tripartite structure** optimizes readability and organization. Clicking these areas activates a specialized ribbon tab, offering options to insert **page numbers**, **timestamps**, and **sheet names** across all pages. This functionality leverages Excel's **dynamic field system**, which updates content automatically based on document properties and user-defined variables.

*Pro tip: Excel's header and footer image insertion process differs from standard clipboard operations. You cannot add an image to the header or footer in Excel by using the keyboard shortcuts Ctrl (or Command) C and Ctrl (or Command) V. Users must employ the **Picture tool** in the ribbon, which interfaces with Excel's **embedded object system**. Image resizing is controlled through the **Format Picture** dialog, utilizing a **parametric resizing algorithm** that maintains image integrity while adapting to header/footer constraints.*

Page Layout View

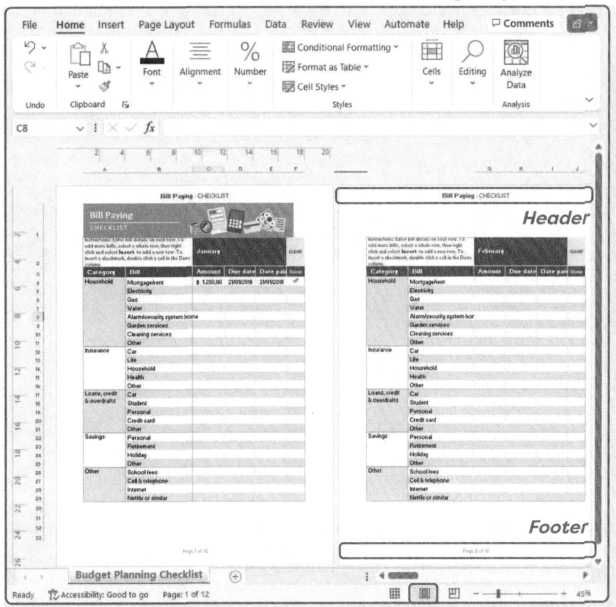

Page Break Preview

The **Page Break Preview** mode is instrumental in **defining print areas** and optimizing output. Content-filled areas are enclosed by **blue lines**, demarcating the printable region. Empty areas appear as a gray screen. Users can manually adjust these blue lines to customize the print area, overriding Excel's automatic margin calculations.

This feature allows for flexible output configuration, such as fitting content to a single page or distributing it across multiple pages. Excel suggests optimal breaks with **blue dashed**

lines, which users can reposition. The **Home tab** offers a print simulation option for verification. It's crucial to note that content outside the blue lines will be excluded from printing or PDF export.

Page Break Preview

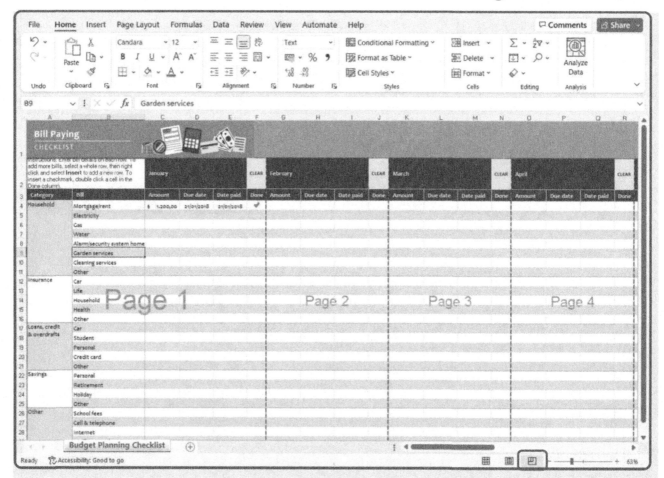

Pro tip: *For multi-worksheet printing, use the **Ctrl** (or **Command**) key while selecting worksheet tabs. This action leverages Excel's **batch processing capabilities**, allowing simultaneous configuration of multiple sheets.*

*The **File tab's print view** will display all selected worksheets, enabling efficient bulk printing. This feature utilizes Excel's **document object model** to treat multiple worksheets as a single printable unit, streamlining the output process for complex workbooks.*

Print View

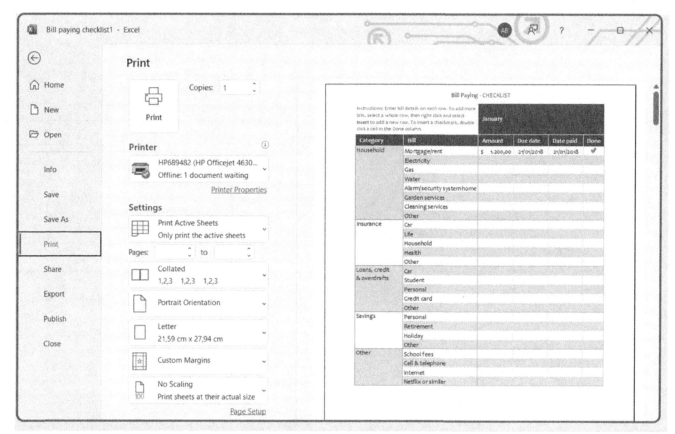

Formatting Cells

Mastering cell formatting is crucial for effective Excel use. While basic formatting was covered in Chapter 1, we'll now delve into Excel-specific features.

Numeric and Stylistic Formatting

The **Home tab** houses the **Number section**, offering quick formatting options and an expanded dialog box. We recommend initially using the dialog box for a comprehensive view. Remember to **select target cells before formatting**.

The dialog box presents various **data type options**, crucial for accurate calculations. Choices range from time formats to custom styles. Exploring each option familiarizes you with Excel's capabilities. Additional formatting options include alignment, font, border, fill, and cell protection.

Home Tab

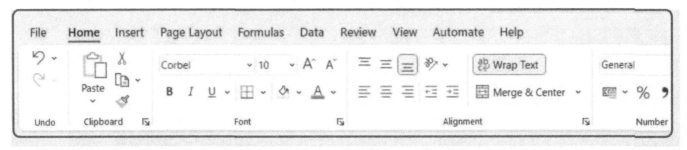

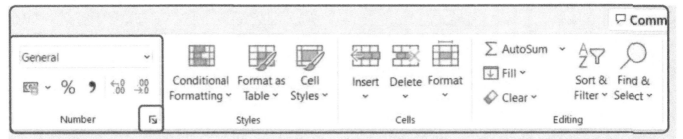

Number section

Pro tip: *To* **safeguard data integrity** *when sharing spreadsheets, utilize the* **cell locking feature**. *Access this in the* **Protection tab** *of the formatting dialog box.*

To complete the process, navigate to the **Review tab** *and select* **Protect Sheet**. *This prompts you to set permissions and create a* **password**, *establishing a robust security measure for sensitive data.*

Dialog Box >Protection Tab

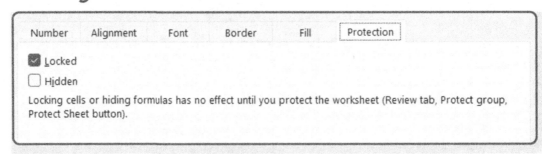

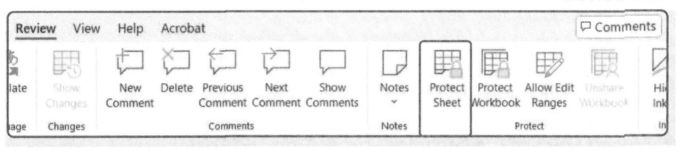

Conditional Formatting: Dinamic Rules

Conditional Formatting is a powerful tool for automating cell appearance based on content. Access this feature via the Home tab. Select **New Rule** to open a dialog box where you can define formatting criteria. For instance, choose **Format cells that contain** to set specific conditions.

After establishing rules, click **Format** to determine the visual representation of qualifying cells. Remember to **pre-select target cells** before applying conditional formatting.

Excel offers various preset conditional formatting options, including **color scales**, **icon sets**, **data bars**, and **ranking systems**. These tools leverage Excel's powerful **data visualization capabilities**, transforming raw numbers into easily interpretable visual patterns.

To manage or review existing rules, return to the Conditional Formatting menu. This centralized control allows for efficient rule modification and removal, ensuring your spreadsheet remains organized and visually coherent.

Excel's formatting capabilities extend beyond basic aesthetics. The software employs sophisticated **algorithms** to analyze data patterns and apply formatting dy-

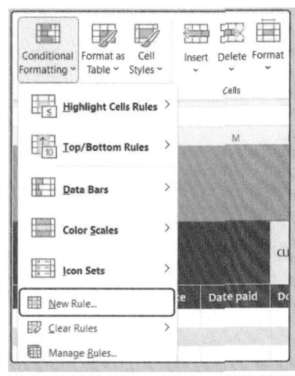

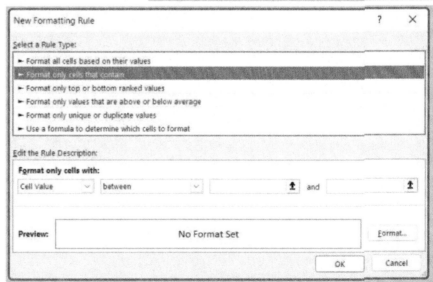

namically. For instance, the **Top/Bottom Rules** feature uses statistical analysis to highlight extreme values automatically.

Furthermore, Excel's **custom formula** option in conditional formatting allows for complex, multi-criteria rules. This feature essentially turns every cell into a potential micro-program, capable of making formatting decisions based on intricate logical conditions.

Advanced Formatting Techniques and Tips and Tricks

Once you've mastered cell management, Excel's other features become more accessible. Here are some **valuable formatting tips**:

- **Leverage the paintbrush:** This tool efficiently applies formatting across multiple cells. For detailed usage, refer to Chapter 1's formatting section.

- **Automate Series or Repetitions:** Instead of manual input or copy-pasting, use Excel's autofill feature. Locate the fill handle (a small cross) in the cell's bottom-right corner. Drag it to automatically extend content or formatting. A smart tag appears after release, offering options like series continuation or format-only replication.

- **Cell Relocation:** To move cell contents, select the cell and hover over its border until a **four-arrow cursor** appears. Click and drag to the desired location. This action preserves formatting and formulas.

Pro tip: When relocating cells involved in formulas, be cautious. The move may alter calculation results. Review and adjust formulas in affected cells to maintain accuracy.

- **Date Formatting Nuances:** Excel's date handling can be confusing. Unformatted date entries may appear as numbers, representing days since January 1, 1900. To display dates correctly, ensure cells use the **Date format**. The default format is day/month/year, customizable in the **Number Format dialog.**

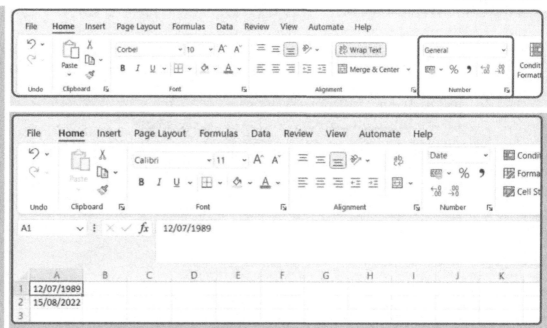

- **Text Wrapping and Line Breaks:** For multi-line text within a cell, use **Alt+Enter** while typing in the formula bar (**fx**). Alternatively, the **Wrap Text** function in the **Alignment** section automatically adjusts text to fit column width.

Pro tip: *You can also use the **Wrap text** function in the **Alignment** section of the home tab to have the cell automatically adjust to its content. This will automatically **adjust the content** to the current column width of the spreadsheet and increase the line spacing. If you use the tip in the **line break section**, the cells will format themselves automatically.*

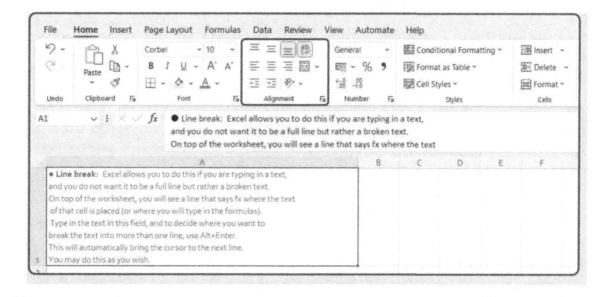

Excel's Computational Core: Formulas and Functions

We now delve into Excel's most crucial feature: **formulas**. These powerful tools drive Excel's calculation capabilities and are accessible through three primary methods:

1. **Manual entry** in the formula bar
2. Using the **Function Library** in the Formulas tab
3. Utilizing the *fx* button for guided formula creation

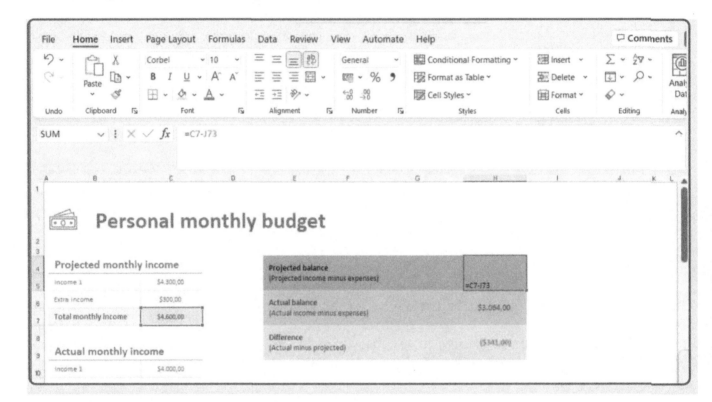

When **manually inputting formulas**, remember they must begin with a mathematical symbol. The **equal sign (=)** is most common, but **plus (+)** and **minus (-)** are also valid. Note that **asterisk (*)** for multiplication and **forward slash (/)** for division cannot initiate formulas.

> **Pro tip:** *To display text beginning with '+', '-', or '=', prefix it with an **apostrophe (')**. This invisible character prevents Excel from interpreting the text as a formula, ensuring accurate display without affecting printed output.*

Excel's formula capabilities extend beyond cell references. You can perform **direct calculations** by entering expressions like =5+7+9. This feature allows for quick, one-off calculations without occupying additional cells.

Hint: *While Excel offers a vast library of pre-built functions, don't hesitate to craft* **custom formulas** *tailored to your specific needs. This flexibility allows you to leverage Excel's computational power for unique problem-solving.*

Remember, effective formula use goes beyond mere calculation. It's about **structuring your data logically** and **creating dynamic, responsive spreadsheets**. As you master formulas, you'll find Excel transforming from a simple grid into a powerful analytical tool, capable of handling complex business scenarios and data-driven decision-making processes.

AutoSum: Essential Calculations at Your Fingertips

The **AutoSum feature** in Excel provides quick access to five fundamental functions: **sum, average, count number, maximum, and minimum**. Located in both the **Home** and **Formulas** tabs, AutoSum streamlines basic data analysis.

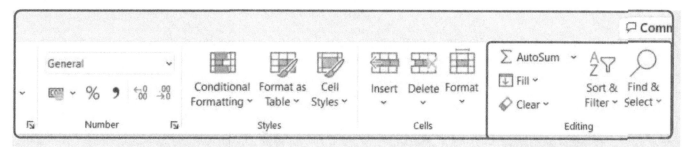

Let's explore these functions using a sample dataset: 6, 15, 1, 27, 9, 3, 65, 87, 41, 2, 7 (in cells B1 through B11).

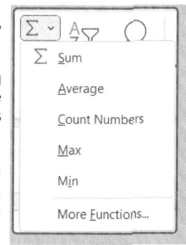

- **Sum**: Calculates the total of selected values. The first thing we'll do is add these numbers together. Select the cell where you want the result to appear and click on the AutoSum icon's **Sum** element.

  If the cell you chose is directly beneath the numbers or on cell **B12,** it will automatically select the interval directly above it, or B1-B11. If the system does not select it automatically, you can do it manually. Keep in mind that the following formula will appear on the top bar: **=sum(B1:B11).**

  This will result in the following: Excel will compute the sum of the values in cells B1 through B11. When you've finished selecting the cells you want to add, press enter, and the result will appear automatically: **263.**

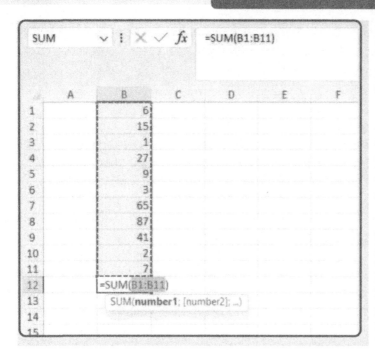
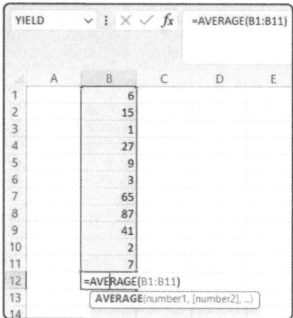

- **Average:** Computes the arithmetic mean. The average function will have the same selection requirements as the sum function. However, in this case, the formula that will appear is: **=average(B1:B11).** This will result in the following once more: Excel will compute the average of the numbers **in cells B1 through B11**. You will click Enter once more (as you will for all formulas) and the result will appear: 23.90909.

> **Pro tip:** *Control decimal places displayed by using the **Increase Decimal** and **Decrease Decimal** buttons in the **Number** section of the **Home** tab. This affects display only, not the underlying value.*

- **Count number:** Tallies the quantity of numeric entries. It is convenient to see the number of occurrences without having to manually count or perform calculations. **=count(B1:B11)** will be the formula. In this case, the answer is 11.

- **Maximum:** Identifies the highest value. Formula **=max(B1:B11)**. The answer in our case is 87.

- **Minimum:** This, like the previous example, determines the minimum value within the range. The formula is as follows: **=min(B1:B11).** The answer to the proposed example is 1.

> **Pro tip:** *Excel's formulas can handle multiple data sets simultaneously. While our examples used a single range (B1:B11), you can easily expand this to include additional data. For instance, to incorporate numbers from column D, rows 7-13, you'll need to modify your formula.*

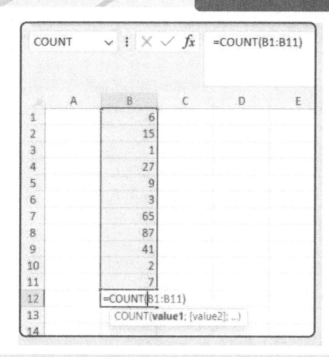

*To select non-adjacent ranges, hold down the **Ctrl key** (or **Command** on Mac) while click-ing each range. Excel will automatically separate these ranges with a **comma (,)** in the formula. For example, to find the maximum value across both ranges, your formula would look like this: **=MAX(B1:B11,D7:D13)***

This powerful feature allows you to perform calculations on dispersed data without need-ing separate formulas for each range.

Remember: *Precision is key when writing formulas. Avoid using spaces within the formula, as this can lead to errors. Excel's formula syntax is designed to be compact and space-free for optimal functionality.*

Financial Formulas

Excel is a powerful tool for financial management, widely used by both businesses and in-dividuals to monitor and analyze their finances. The software offers a robust set of financial formulas that cater to various financial calculations and projections.

In this section, we'll explore five of the most crucial financial formulas that Excel provides. These tools are essential for tasks such as budgeting, investment analysis, and financial planning.

For those seeking a more comprehensive list of financial functions, Excel's **Formulas** tab contains a dedicated **Financial** button. This feature opens up a wealth of additional finan-

cial formulas, allowing users to perform complex financial analyses tailored to their specific needs.

Whether you're a small business owner tracking cash flow, an investor analyzing potential returns, or an individual managing personal finances, mastering these Excel financial functions can significantly enhance your financial decision-making process. Let's dive into these powerful financial tools that Excel puts at your fingertips.

Formulas Tab

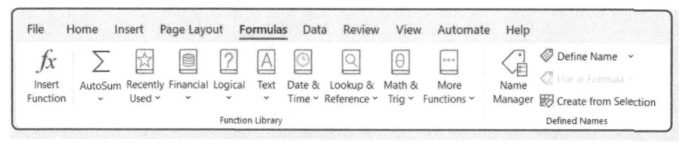

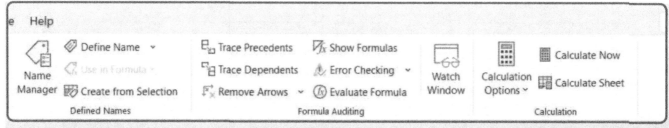

- **YIELD:** The **YIELD** function in Excel calculates the return on an investment over a specified period, accommodating both periodic and single payments. Here's a breakdown of its components:

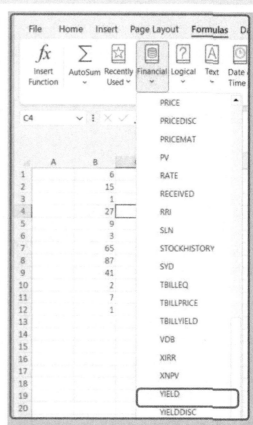

  - **Settlement date**: Input as a serial date number (e.g., 44,566 for 05/01/2022).

  - **Maturity date**: Also entered as a serial date (e.g., 45,299 for 08/01/2024).

  - **Annual coupon rate**: Expressed as a decimal (e.g., 0.06 for 6%).

  - **Pr (Price)**: The security's price per $100 face value (e.g., $105).

  - **Redemption value**: Per $100 face value (e.g., $140).

  - **Frequency**: Payment periodicity (e.g., 2 for semi-annual).

- **Basis**: Day count basis (e.g., 3).

Your yield computation will provide a result of 20%. The final formula will be as follows:

=YIELD(44566,45299,0.06,105,140,2,3)

Remember that, while you can manually enter these numbers, you can alternatively create a table that looks like this:

The formula would look like this: **=YIELD(L14,L15,L16,L17,L18,2,3)**

	K	L
14	*Settlement date:*	05/01/2022
15	*Maturity date:*	08/01/2024
16	*Rate of interest:*	6%
17	*Price per $100 FV:*	105
18	*Redemption value:*	140
19	*Payment terms*	Semi-annual

Pro tip: When utilizing this formula, you might encounter '#NUM!' or '#VALUE!' errors, indicating incorrect formula inputs. The '#VALUE!' error often suggests that an argument isn't numeric or that settlement or maturity dates are invalid.

Conversely, a '#NUM!' error could mean the settlement date is equal to or greater than the maturity date, or that invalid numbers were entered for an argument. These error messages serve as crucial indicators that your formula inputs need review and correction.

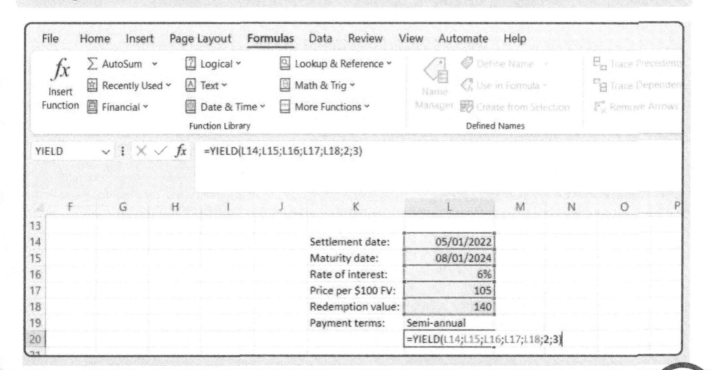

- **PRICE:** Let's explore a scenario where you know the yield but need to determine a security's price. Excel provides a formula for this calculation as well. We'll use the same figures from our previous example, but instead of the face value, we'll incorporate the yield into our calculation.

  The formula structure will be: **=PRICE(44566,45299,0.06,0.2,140,2,3)**

  This computation yields a result of $105, which aligns perfectly with the face value we used in our initial example, confirming the accuracy of our calculation. As before, we can organize this information in a tabular format for clarity and ease of reference. The table layout would be similar to our previous example, with the yield replacing the face value entry.

	K	L
14	*Settlement date:*	05/01/2022
15	*Maturity date:*	08/01/2024
16	*Rate of interest:*	6%
17	*Yield:*	20%
18	*Redemption value:*	140
19	*Payment terms*	Semi-annual

  And the formula will be this: **=PRICE(L14,L15,L16,L17,L18,2,3)**

- **RATE:** The RATE function in Excel proves invaluable when determining the interest rate for a potential loan. This formula requires several key inputs. First, you need the Nper, which represents the total number of payment periods. For a two-year loan, this would be 24 months. Next is the Pmt, the fixed monthly payment, entered as a negative number.

  In our example, it's -$351. The Pv represents the principal amount of the loan, which in this case is $6,000. The Fv, or future value, is typically used for investments rather than loans, so we'll use 0. The Type specifies whether payments are made at the beginning (1) or end (0) of the period. For loans, we'll use 0. Lastly, the Guess is an initial estimate of the interest rate, expressed as a decimal. We'll use 0.1 (10%).The final formula will look like this, and the answer will be 3%:

  The complete formula looks like this: **=RATE(24,-351,6000,0,0,0.1)**

This returns a result of 3%, representing the monthly interest rate. You can also organize this information in an Excel table with columns K and L. Column K would list the parameters: Payment, Loan amount, Monthly payment, Number of months, and Payments per year. Column L would contain the corresponding values: Monthly, 6,000, 351, 24, and 12.

	K	L
10	*Payment:*	Monthly
11	*Loan amount:*	6,000
12	*Monthly payment:*	351
13	*Number of months:*	24
14	*Payments per year:*	12

Using cell references, the formula would be: **=RATE(L13,-L12,L11,0,0,0.1)**

This approach allows for easy adjustments to the loan parameters, making it simple to calculate interest rates for various scenarios.

- **NOMINAL**: The nominal function in Excel is a straightforward yet powerful tool for calculating the annual nominal interest rate of a loan or financial application. This formula is relatively simple, requiring only two inputs to generate its result.

The first input is the **Effect_rate,** which represents the effective interest rate of the application. In our example, we'll use 16%, or 0.16 when expressed as a decimal. This rate reflects the actual annual rate of interest when compounding is taken into account.

The second input is the **Npery number,** which stands for the number of compounding periods per year. If we want to calculate the nominal rate on an annual basis, we would input 12, representing monthly compounding over a year. With these two pieces of information, we can construct our nominal function in Excel.

The formula would look like this: **=NOMINAL(0.16, 12)**

When we enter this formula, Excel calculates and returns the annual nominal interest rate. In this case, the result is 15%.

This 15% represents the stated annual interest rate without taking into account the effects of compounding. It's important to note that while the effective rate (16%) accounts for compounding, the nominal rate (15%) does not, which explains why it's slightly lower.

- **Variable Declining Balance (VDB)**: This formula is a powerful tool for calculating asset depreciation over a specific period. Let's break down how to use this formula to determine the daily depreciation of a car.

To begin, you'll need several key pieces of information. First, you'll input the **cost of the asset,** which in this case is the purchase price of the car at $15,000. Next, you'll need to estimate the salvage value, or what the car might be worth after a year. For our example, we'll use $13,000 as the salvage value.

The life value of the asset is the estimated time it will be used, which we've set at 10 years. Since we want to calculate the depreciation per day, we'll convert this to days by multiplying by 365.

The start period in this scenario is 0, representing the day you buy the car. The end period is 1, as we're looking at the depreciation for a single day. The factor, which represents the rate of decline, can be left at 1 if you choose to omit it.

Putting all this together, our VDB formula looks like this: **=VDB(15000,13000,10*365,0,1)**

When we enter this formula into Excel, it returns a result of $8.22. This means the car will depreciate by $8.22 per day from the day of purchase. To organize this information in a table format, you could set it up as follows:

	K	L
10	*Initial cost:*	15.000
11	*Salvage:*	13.000
12	*Life:*	10 years

Using cell references, the formula would then be: **=VDB(L10,L11,L12*365,0,1)**

This approach allows for easy adjustments to the parameters, making it simple to calculate depreciation for various scenarios or assets.

Logical Formulas

Logical formulas in Excel are indeed powerful tools for combining multiple conditions or calculations. They allow users to perform complex operations without the need for multiple separate formulas across different cells. Here's an overview of these useful functions:

Logical Formulas

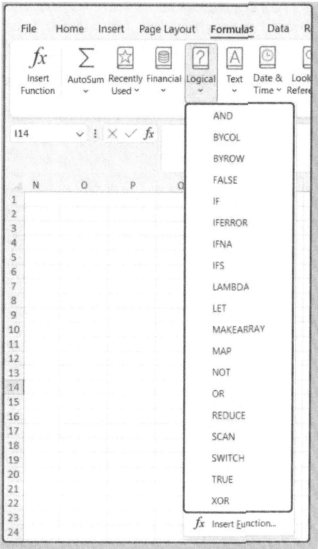

- **AND**: The **AND formula** will be used to join two or more logical references. The AND function evaluates whether all specified conditions are true. It returns TRUE only if every condition within the function is true. If any condition is false, the entire function returns FALSE.

For example:

=AND(1>2, 2>1) This returns FALSE because while 2>1 is true, 1>2 is false. Since not all conditions are true, the result is FALSE.

=AND(3>2, 2>1) This returns TRUE because both 3>2 and 2>1 are true. All conditions are met, so the result is TRUE.

The AND function can handle more than two conditions.

For instance: **=AND(A1>10, B1<20, C1=15)**

This would return TRUE only if all three conditions are met: A1 is greater than 10, B1 is less than 20, and C1 equals 15.

You can input conditions manually, as in the examples above, or reference cell values.

For instance: **=AND(A1>B1, C1=D1)**

This checks if the value in A1 is greater than B1 and if C1 equals D1.

- **OR**: The **OR function** in Excel is another powerful logical formula that works similarly to AND, but with a key difference in how it evaluates conditions. Here's a detailed explanation of the OR function:

The OR function checks if any of the provided conditions are true. It returns TRUE if at least one condition is true, and FALSE only if all conditions are false.

For example:

=OR(1>2, 2>1) This returns TRUE because while 1>2 is false, 2>1 is true. Since at least one condition is true, the result is TRUE.

=OR(1>2, 3<2) This returns FALSE because both conditions (1>2 and 3<2) are false. Since all conditions are false, the result is FALSE.

The OR function can handle multiple conditions: **=OR(A1>10, B1<20, C1=15)**

This would return TRUE if any of these conditions are met: A1 is greater than 10, or B1 is less than 20, or C1 equals 15.

Like AND, you can use cell references or manual inputs: **=OR(A1="Yes", B1="Maybe", C1="Possibly")**

This would return TRUE if any of the cells A1, B1, or C1 contain "Yes", "Maybe", or "Possibly". You can also combine OR with other functions, including AND, to create more complex logical tests.

For instance: **=OR(AND(A1>0, A1<10), AND(B1>0, B1<10))**

This would return TRUE if either A1 or B1 is between 0 and 10.

- **IFERROR:** The **IFERROR function** in Excel is a valuable tool for error handling and improving the readability of your spreadsheets. Here's a detailed explanation of how it works:

IFERROR evaluates an expression and returns a specified value if the expression results in an error. If there's no error, it returns the result of the expression.

The basic syntax is: **=IFERROR(value, value_if_error)**

For example:

=IFERROR(12/0, "incorrect") This returns "incorrect" because 12/0 results in a #DIV/0! error.

=IFERROR(L15, "incorrect") If L15 contains a formula that results in an error (like #NUM!, #VALUE!, #REF!, #NAME?, etc.), this will return "incorrect". If L15 doesn't contain an error, it will return the value in L15.

IFERROR can handle various error types, including:

- **#DIV/0!** (division by zero)
- **#N/A** (value not available)
- **#NAME?** (unrecognized formula name)
- **#NULL!** (invalid cell reference)
- **#NUM!** (invalid numeric value)
- **#REF!** (invalid cell reference)

- **#VALUE!** (wrong type of argument in a function or formula)

Some practical uses of IFERROR include:

1. Cleaning up spreadsheet appearance by replacing error messages with blank cells: **=IFERROR(formula, "")**

2. Providing custom error messages: **=IFERROR(VLOOKUP(A1, B:C, 2, FALSE), "Not found")**

3. Performing alternative calculations when the primary calculation fails: **=IFER-ROR(1/A1, 0)**

Pro tip: As mentioned, when you want to return text as the error value, you must enclose it in quotation marks. However, if you're returning a number or a cell reference as the error value, quotation marks are not needed.

- **COUNTIF:** The **COUNTIF function** in Excel is indeed a powerful tool for analyzing data and counting occurrences of specific values within a range. Here's a detailed explanation of how it works:

COUNTIF syntax: =COUNTIF(range, criteria)

In the example you provided: **=COUNTIF(B4:B17,1)**

The range is B4:B17, which contains the list of numbers: 6, 15, 1, 27, 9, 1, 3, 65, 87, 1, 41, 2, and 7.

The criteria is 1, which is the value we're counting. This formula would return 3, as the number 1 appears three times in the given range. Key points about COUNTIF:

1. It can count numbers, text, or logical values (TRUE/FALSE).

2. For text criteria, you need to use quotation marks. For example: =COUNTIF(A1:A10, "Apple")

3. You can use wildcards with text: **=COUNTIF(A1:A10, "A*")** would count all cells starting with "A"

4. For numerical criteria, you can use comparison operators: **=COUNTIF(B4:B17, ">10")** would count numbers greater than 10

5. You can reference a cell for the criteria: **=COUNTIF(B4:B17, D1)** where D1 contains the value you're counting

6. **COUNTIF** is case-insensitive for text.

COUNTIF can handle large datasets efficiently, making it invaluable when dealing with extensive information that would be time-consuming to analyze manually. It's a versatile tool that can be used across various types of data analysis tasks in Excel.

*   **IF**: The **IF function** is one of Excel's most powerful and widely used tools. It allows you to make logical decisions in your spreadsheets. Let's break it down with a simple example. The IF function has three parts:

    1. A logical test (is something true or false?)
    2. What to do if the test is true
    3. What to do if the test is false

Here's the basic structure: **=IF(logical_test, value_if_true, value_if_false)**

Let's use a simple math example:

Example 1: =IF(1>2, "CORRECT", "RECALCULATE")

Here's what's happening:

*   Excel checks if 1 is greater than 2 (which it isn't)
*   Since it's false, Excel returns "RECALCULATE"

Example 2: =IF(2>1, "CORRECT", "RECALCULATE")

In this case: Excel checks if 2 is greater than 1 (which it is). Since it's true, Excel returns "CORRECT"

Pro Tip for Beginners: *You can use cell references instead of numbers in your IF statements. For example, =IF(A1>B1, "A1 is bigger", "B1 is bigger or equal")*

Understanding Cell References

When you copy formulas in Excel, the cell references usually change. This is called relative referencing. But sometimes, you want a reference to stay the same. That's where absolute referencing comes in.

Here's how it works:

1. **Relative Reference:** A1, B2, etc. These change when you copy the formula.
2. **Absolute Reference:** $A$1, $B$2, etc. These stay the same when you copy the formula.
3. **Mixed Reference:** $A1 or A$1. One part stays the same, the other changes.

Example:

- Let's say you have **=SUM(A1:A7)** in cell **B1**, and you want to copy it down to **B2:B5**.
- Without $ signs, it would change to **=SUM(A2:A8)** in **B2**, **=SUM(A3:A9) in B3**, and so on.
- With $ signs like this: **=SUM($A$1:$A$7)**, it would stay the same in all cells.

Step-by-step to use absolute references:

1. Type your formula normally
2. Place your cursor on the cell reference you want to lock
3. Press F4 to cycle through reference types ($A$1 → A$1 → $A1 → A1)

Remember, $ before the letter locks the column, $ before the number locks the row.

Pro Tip: *Understanding when to use relative, absolute, or mixed references is key to creating flexible and powerful Excel formulas. Practice with different scenarios to master this concept!*

Text Formulas

- **CLEAN**: The CLEAN function removes non-printable characters from text in your spreadsheet. It's useful for cleaning up data copied from other sources. **=CLEAN(text)**

Example: If A1 contains: "Hello World" (with extra hidden characters)

=CLEAN(A1) would result in: "Hello World" (without hidden characters)

Note: CLEAN doesn't remove visible spaces. To remove all spaces, use:

=SUBSTITUTE(CLEAN(A1), " ", "")

This combines CLEAN (to remove non-printable characters) with SUBSTITUTE (to remove spaces).

Remember: *Always test on a copy of your data first!*

Text Formulas

- **CONCATENATE**: This **function** is a powerful tool in Excel that allows you to combine text from multiple cells or strings into a single cell. This function is particularly useful when you need to merge data from different columns or create custom text strings.

The basic structure of the CONCATENATE function is:

=CONCATENATE(text1, [text2], …)

Where:

- text1 is required and can be text, a cell reference, or a formula that results in text.

- [text2] and beyond are optional additional items you want to join.

Examples and Use Cases:

1. **Joining Numbers from Different Cells:** Let's say you have numbers in cells C4, C7, and C11, and you want to combine them:

=CONCATENATE(C4,C7,C11) If C4=1, C7=2, C11=3, the result would be "123"

2. **Combining Words:** If you have words in different cells or want to join text strings:

=CONCATENATE("CAR","DRIVE","ROAD") This would result in: CARDRIVEROAD

3. **Adding Spaces and Punctuation:** To make the combined text more readable, you can add spaces and punctuation:

=CONCATENATE("CAR ", "DRIVE. ", "ROAD!") This would give: CAR DRIVE. ROAD!

4. **Mixing Cell References and Text:** You can combine cell references with fixed text: If A1 contains "Excel" and B1 contains "fun":

=CONCATENATE("Learning ", A1, " is ", B1, "!") This would result in: Learning Excel is fun!

Pro Tips:

1. *Remember to include spaces within the quotes if you want spaces between words.*
2. *You can use CONCATENATE to create custom formulas, like combining first and last names, or building email addresses.*
3. *In newer versions of Excel, you can use the & operator instead of CONCATENATE: ="CAR " & "DRIVE " & "ROAD" is equivalent to =CONCATENATE("CAR ", "DRIVE ", "ROAD")*

- **REPLACE:** The REPLACE function in Excel does exactly what its name implies. It allows you to substitute one value for another using a formula. Here's how it works:

  1. Choose the "old text" - the original text you want to modify (e.g., FALSE).

  2. Specify the "start_num" - the position where you want to begin the replacement (e.g., 5 for the 'E' in FALSE).

  3. Determine the "num_chars" - how many characters you want to replace (e.g., 1).

  4. Enter the "new text" - what you want to insert (e.g., 3).

  The formula structure is: **=REPLACE(old_text, start_num, num_chars, new_text)**

  For our example: =REPLACE(FALSE,5,1,3)

  This yields 'FALS3' as the result. The REPLACE function is particularly useful when you need to change multiple characters in lengthy text or across a large dataset within your spreadsheet.

- **SEARCH:** The **SEARCH function** in Excel helps users locate a specific value within a cell or range of cells. Here's a breakdown of how it works:

  1. It's not case-sensitive, treating uppercase and lowercase letters the same.

  2. The formula structure is: **=SEARCH(find_text, within_text, [start_num])**

     - **find_text:** The text you're looking for
     - **within_text:** The text you're searching within
     - **start_num:** Optional; where to start the search (defaults to 1 if omitted)

3. For example, let's search for 'A' in "THE CAR IS DRIVING DOWN THE ROAD": =SEARCH("A","THECARISDRIVINGDOWNTHEROAD",1)

4. The result is 5, because 'A' first appears in the 5th position of the sentence.

This function is particularly useful for finding the position of a character or substring within a larger text string. It can help with text analysis, data cleaning, or as part of more complex formulas in Excel.

- **FIND:** The **FIND function** in Excel is similar to SEARCH, but with a key difference:

  1. FIND is case-sensitive, distinguishing between uppercase and lowercase letters.

  2. The formula structure is: =FIND(find_text, within_text, [start_num])

    - **find_text:** The text you're searching for
    - **within_text:** The text you're searching within
    - **start_num:** Optional; where to start the search (defaults to 1 if omitted)

  3. For example, searching for 'A' in "THE CAR IS DRIVING DOWN THE ROAD":

  =FIND("A","THECARISDRIVINGDOWNTHEROAD",1)

  4. The result is 5, as 'A' first appears in the 5th position of the sentence.

  5. However, if we search for lowercase 'a':

  =FIND("a","THECARISDRIVINGDOWNTHEROAD",1)

This would return a '#VALUE!' error because there's no lowercase 'a' in the sentence.

The FIND function is useful when you need to locate text with exact case matching, making it more precise than SEARCH in certain situations. It's particularly helpful in data analysis where case sensitivity matters, such as working with codes or identifiers.

Date and Time Formulas

Date and time formulas in Excel may seem simple when used manually, but their true value becomes apparent when handling data structured in rows and columns, sorted by years, months, and days. These formulas offer more than just basic functionality; they provide useful features that allow your document to update automatically on a daily basis, removing the need for manual updates.

This automation streamlines your workflow and ensures your data remains current without constant intervention.

The following sections will explore various date and time formulas that can enhance your Excel experience and improve data management efficiency.

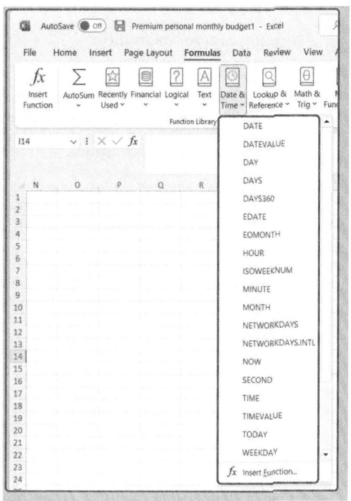

Date and Time Formulas

- **DATE:** The **DATE formula** in Excel is indeed a powerful tool for working with dates, especially when dealing with data organized by year, month, and day. Here's a breakdown of how it works:

  1. The basic structure of the DATE formula is:

     =DATE(YEAR, MONTH, DAY)

  2. It's particularly useful when you have separate columns for year, month, and day.

  3. For example, if you have:

     - Year in column B
     - Month in column C
     - Day in column D

  Your formula would look like this:

  =DATE(B5,C5,D5)

  4. This formula combines the separate components into a single, formatted date.

  5. You can drag this formula down to apply it to multiple rows, automatically updating for each new set of year, month, and day values.

  6. The result will be in Excel's standard date format, which you can then customize as needed.

- **TODAY:** The TODAY function in Excel is a simple yet powerful tool for automatic date tracking. Here's an overview:

Formula and functionality:

- Structure: **=TODAY()**
- Displays the current date in the cell
- Automatically updates when the workbook is opened

Key benefits and applications:

- Eliminates manual date entry
- Ideal for daily updated documents requiring printing
- Useful for tracking spreadsheet access or modifications

The TODAY function is particularly valuable for maintaining current dates in reports, logs, or any document that needs to reflect the most recent date without manual intervention. It can be combined with other formulas for date-based calculations and formatted to display the date in your preferred style, making it a versatile tool for various Excel tasks.

- **TIME:** The TIME function in Excel is similar to the DATE function, but focuses on hours, minutes, and seconds instead of days, months, and years.

Formula structure: =TIME(HOUR,MINUTE,SECOND)

Usage:

- Enter the corresponding values for hour, minute, and second
- Can be used with cell references, like **=TIME(A1,B1,C1)**

Pro tip: Ensure cells are formatted for time display. Select cells and use the Number section in the Home tab. Choose from various time formats based on your needs

Remember, both DATE and TIME functions work similarly, so mastering one makes it easier to use the other. The key is to properly format your cells to display the results correctly, which can greatly enhance the readability and functionality of your spreadsheet.

- **NETWORKDAYS**: The NETWORKDAYS function in Excel is a useful tool for calculating the number of workdays between two dates:

Formula structure: =NETWORKDAYS(START_DATE, END_DATE, [HOLIDAYS])

Key components:

- **START_DATE:** The beginning of your period
- **END_DATE:** The end of your period
- **[HOLIDAYS]:** Optional; a range of dates to exclude as holidays

Usage:

- Dates should be in serial number format (Excel's internal date representation)
- The function automatically excludes weekends
- Returns the number of workdays in the specified period

This function is particularly valuable for project planning, payroll calculations, or any task requiring knowledge of working days in a given timeframe. It saves time by automatically accounting for weekends and allows for customization by including holidays, making it a powerful tool for business-related date calculations in Excel.

- **YEAR**: The YEAR function in Excel is a straightforward tool for extracting the year from a date:

Formula structure: =YEAR(SERIAL_NUMBER)

Key points:

- Input can be a serial number representing a date
- Also works with dates in standard Excel date format
- Returns only the year as a four-digit number

Usage:

- Useful for converting dates to just their year component
- Helpful in data analysis and reporting
- Can be combined with other functions for more complex date calculations

This function is particularly valuable when you need to isolate the year from a full date, simplifying data organization and analysis. It's commonly used in financial reports, trend analysis, and any scenario where grouping data by year is beneficial.

Reference Formulas

Reference formulas in Excel, including the famous VLOOKUP, are powerful tools often used in corporate environments. While they might sound intimidating, they're actually quite accessible once you understand them. Here's a more approachable take on these formulas:

VLOOKUP and other reference formulas allow you to search and retrieve data across different sheets or even entire workbooks. They're like Excel's built-in detectives, helping you find and connect information quickly.

The reputation of VLOOKUP as being complex is often overstated. With a bit of practice, you'll find it's a user-friendly and incredibly useful tool. It's designed to make your data management tasks easier, not harder.

These formulas are particularly valuable when dealing with large datasets or when you need to pull information from various sources within your spreadsheets.

They can save you significant time and reduce errors that might occur with manual data entry or searching.

Lookup & Reference Formulas

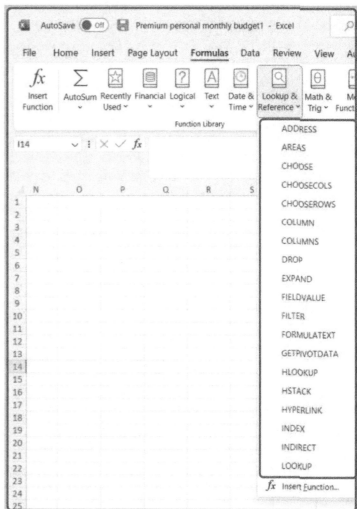

- **HLOOKUP**:

  The HLOOKUP function in Excel is indeed a less commonly used but equally powerful sibling of VLOOKUP. Here's a breakdown of how it works:

Purpose:

- Searches horizontally across the top row of a table
- Returns a value from the same column in a specified row

Formula structure:

=HLOOKUP(lookup_value, table_array, row_index_num, [range_lookup])

Components:

1. **lookup_value**: What you're searching for (e.g., "March")

2. **table_array**: The range containing your data (e.g., A1:L10)

3. **row_index_num**: Which row to return the value from (e.g., 3)

4. **range_lookup**: TRUE for approximate match, FALSE for exact match

Example scenario:

- Months listed in row 1 (A1:L1)
- Data extends to row 10
- Searching for "March" in row 1
- Want to return the value from row 3

Formula example: **=HLOOKUP("March",A1:L10,3,FALSE)**

Result: Returns 3 (assuming March is the third column)

HLOOKUP is particularly useful when your data is organized with **categories across the top** and related information in rows below, allowing for efficient **horizontal data retrieval**.

- **VLOOKUP**: This Formula is a powerful Excel function that allows users to **search for a value in a table and return data from a specified column**. Unlike HLOOKUP, which searches horizontally, VLOOKUP searches vertically.

Let's consider an example: Imagine a spreadsheet where **column A (A1:A12) contains the names of the months**. The VLOOKUP formula requires:

1. **Lookup_value**: The value you're searching for (e.g., "March")

2. **Table_array**: The range where the data is located (e.g., A1:L12)

3. **Column_index_num**: The column number from which to return the value (e.g., 5 for column E)

4. **Range_lookup**: TRUE for approximate match, FALSE for exact match

The formula would look like this: **=VLOOKUP("March",A1:L12,5,FALSE).** This would return the number 3, as March is the third month.

> *Pro tip*: *Both VLOOKUP and HLOOKUP are useful for **finding specific information in large datasets**. For instance, you could use these functions to quickly locate a student's grades across multiple subjects without filtering the entire dataset. **The key difference between VLOOKUP and HLOOKUP is the direction of the search**: VLOOKUP searches vertically (in columns), while HLOOKUP searches horizontally (in rows). The choice between them depends on how your data is organized.*

These functions are particularly valuable when dealing with **extensive tables or databases**, allowing you to efficiently retrieve information based on a known value.

- **MATCH**: The **MATCH function** in Excel is used to **find the position of a specific item within a dataset**. It's particularly useful for locating data in large tables. The function requires three main components:

    1. **Lookup_value**: The value you're searching for
    2. **Table_array**: The range of cells containing your data
    3. **Match_type**: A number (1, 0, or -1) that determines how the match is performed

The **match_type** parameter has three options:

- **1**: Finds the **largest value less than or equal** to the lookup value. The array must be in **ascending order**.

- **0**: Finds an **exact match** to the lookup value. The array order doesn't matter.

- **-1**: Finds the **smallest value greater than or equal** to the lookup value. The array must be in **descending order**.

This function is particularly **useful for finding relative positions** of data points within a dataset, which can then be used in other formulas or analyses.

Key points:

- MATCH returns a **position**, not a value
- The **order of your data** is crucial when using match_type 1 or -1
- Use match_type 0 for **exact matches** regardless of data order

- **TRANSPOSE**: is a powerful Excel function that **reorganizes data orientation**. It's particularly useful for **converting data between column and row formats**.

Key features of TRANSPOSE:

- **Column to Row**: It can transform data from a vertical column into a horizontal row.
- **Row to Column**: Conversely, it can change horizontal data into a vertical format.

How to use TRANSPOSE:

1. Select the source data range
2. Choose the destination area where you want the transposed data
3. Enter the formula and press Enter

? — ☐ ✕

The beauty of TRANSPOSE lies in its **simplicity and efficiency**. With just one function, you can **quickly restructure your data layout**, saving time and effort in manual data entry or complex copy-paste operations.

Applications:

- **Data analysis**: Changing data orientation can sometimes reveal new patterns or make analysis easier.

- **Report formatting**: Quickly adjust data presentation for different reporting needs.

- **Data import/export**: Easily modify data structure when moving between different systems or formats.

Pro tip: TRANSPOSE is particularly **useful when working with large datasets** or when you frequently need to switch between horizontal and vertical data presentations.

- **FORMULATEXT**: is a **highly valuable Excel function** that reveals the underlying formulas in cells. It's particularly useful when working with **complex or unfamiliar spreadsheets**.

Key features of FORMULATEXT:

- **Formula Revelation**: It displays the exact formula used in a specified cell.
- **Troubleshooting Aid**: Helps in understanding and debugging complex spreadsheets.

How to use FORMULATEXT:

1. Select an empty cell where you want the formula to be displayed.
2. Enter the FORMULATEXT function, referencing the cell you want to examine.
3. Press Enter to see the formula.

Benefits:

- **Transparency**: Quickly **uncover hidden calculations** in spreadsheets.
- **Learning Tool**: Great for **understanding how complex formulas** are constructed.
- **Auditing**: Useful for **checking and verifying** spreadsheet logic.

*Pro tip: **FORMULATEXT** is especially helpful when inheriting or reviewing spreadsheets created by others. It's like having an X-ray vision for Excel formulas!*

This function **eliminates the guesswork** in deciphering spreadsheet logic, making it an **essential tool for Excel users** of all levels.

Data Validation, Transforming Text, and Filtering

Excel offers powerful tools for managing and organizing data, especially useful when collaborating with others. The chapter's next section explores data validation, text transformation, and filtering. These features help maintain data integrity, standardize information, and improve searchability in shared spreadsheets. Filtering is particularly valuable, allowing users to efficiently sort through large datasets and quickly find specific information.

Data Tab

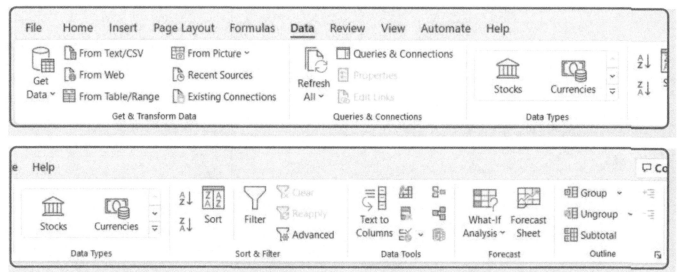

Data Validation

Data validation is a powerful Excel feature that allows you to **control and limit the type of data** users can enter into specific cells. This tool offers various options, including whole numbers, decimals, lists, dates, times, text of a certain length, or custom entries.

For example, you can create a **drop-down list** with predetermined options. To do this, you'll need to:

1. Choose "List" from the validation options
2. Select a **source range** containing your desired values
3. Ensure the source data is accessible to Excel, either on the same sheet or another

Once set up, users will only be able to select from the options in the drop-down menu, **restricting input to predefined values**.

Data validation also allows you to add **custom messages**, such as error alerts for incorrect entries or input instructions when a cell is selected. These features help **guide users** and **maintain data integrity**.

To access and set up data validation, use the **Data Validation button** located in the **Data tab** of the Excel ribbon. This tool is particularly useful for **creating user-friendly forms** and **ensuring data consistency** in shared spreadsheets.

Transforming Text: Text to Columns

Importing data from external sources into Excel can often lead to **formatting issues**, particularly when copying from PDFs. Typically, Excel fails to recognize the **original column structure**, merging all information into a **single line**. To address this, Excel offers the **"Text to Columns"** feature.

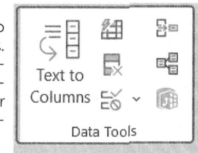

This powerful tool allows users to **split merged data** back into separate columns, effectively restoring the original table format. By using **"Text to Columns,"** you can overcome data import challenges, ensuring your spreadsheet remains a versatile and efficient tool for analysis and management. This feature is crucial for maintaining data integrity and usability when working with information from diverse sources in Excel.

How to Access: Find it in the **Data tab** of the Excel ribbon, under the **"Data Tools" section**.

Step-by-Step Process:

1. **Select Your Data**: Click and drag to highlight the column containing the text you want to split.

2. **Launch Text to Columns**: Click the button in the Data tab.

3. **Choose Data Type**:

   • **Delimited**: For data separated by commas, tabs, spaces, or other characters.
   • **Fixed Width**: For data aligned in columns with spaces between each field.

4. Specify Delimiters (if Delimited):

   • Check boxes for common separators like commas, tabs, or spaces.
   • Use the "Other" box to specify custom delimiters (like semicolons).

5. **Preview**: Excel shows you how your data will look after splitting.

6. **Data Destination**: Choose where you want the split data to appear.

   • Ensure you have enough empty columns to the right of your original data.

7. **Advanced Options**: You can specify column data formats if needed.

8. **Finish**: Click "Finish" to apply the transformation.

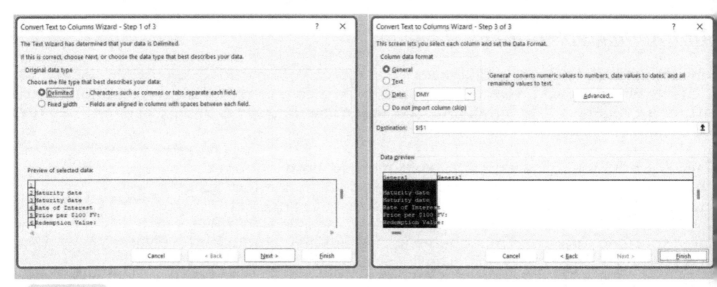

Pro Tips:

1. *Always make a copy of your original data before transforming it.*
2. *Use the Find and Replace tool to clean up any remaining formatting issues.*
3. *For large datasets, consider using Power Query for more advanced transformations.*

This feature is invaluable for **data cleaning and preparation**, making it easier to analyze and work with information from various sources in Excel.

How to Sort and Set Filter

Filtering in Excel is a powerful tool for **data management and analysis**. It allows users to **quickly sort through large datasets** and focus on specific information.

The **"Sort & Filter" button** in the **Home tab** is the gateway to these features. When activated, it adds **dropdown arrows** to each column header, enabling various filtering options:

- **Value filters**: Select or deselect specific data points

- **Color filters**: Sort by cell or font color

- **Number filters**: Include options like "Greater than," "Less than," or "Between"

- **Text filters**: Search for specific text or patterns

- **Date filters**: Narrow down data by time periods

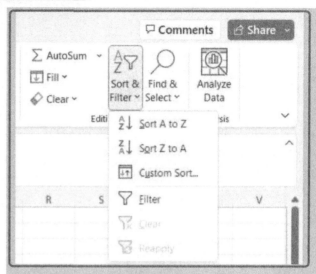

Advanced filtering options allow for more complex criteria, such as filtering based on multiple conditions simultaneously.

Best practices:

- Always use **clear, descriptive headers** for your data columns

- **Regularly clear filters** to ensure you're not missing data

- Use **color coding** strategically to enhance visual filtering

Filters are **dynamically linked** to your data, automatically updating as you make changes. This makes them invaluable for **real-time data analysis** and **report generation**.

Mastering Excel's filtering capabilities can **dramatically improve efficiency** in data handling, making it easier to **identify trends**, **spot anomalies**, and **extract meaningful insights** from your spreadsheets.

Create Pivot Tables

Pivot Tables are the final Excel tool you should know about. They're relatively straightforward, even if you've never used them before. **Pivot tables help organize large datasets** and create dynamic, more accessible visualizations of your data. They're particularly useful when dealing with **thousands of data points** that are difficult to comprehend or relate to. This tool allows you to sort data and even create interactive charts.

Insert Tab

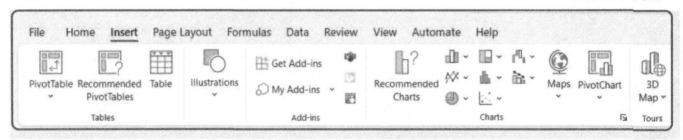

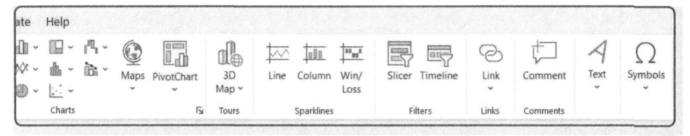

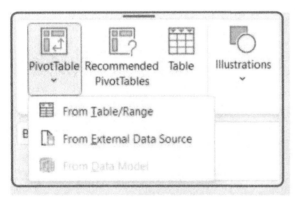

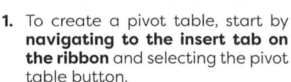

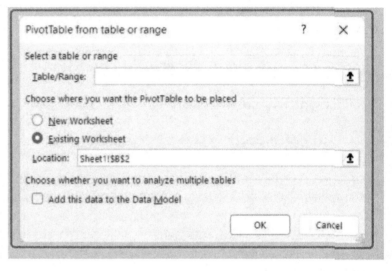

1. To create a pivot table, start by **navigating to the insert tab on the ribbon** and selecting the pivot table button.

2. Choose **PivotTable from the table or range** from the dropdown menu. A dialog box will appear, and your cursor will move to the table/range bar, allowing you to **select the data table** you want to work with.

3. Next, decide whether to place the new pivot table in the current worksheet or a new one (recommended if other worksheets contain information).

4. Finally, simply click "OK" to generate a table with all the data you need.

Pivot Tables in Excel offer a powerful **pro tip** for advanced data analysis. Users can perform additional calculations on the data in the **values field**, enhancing the insights gained from their data.

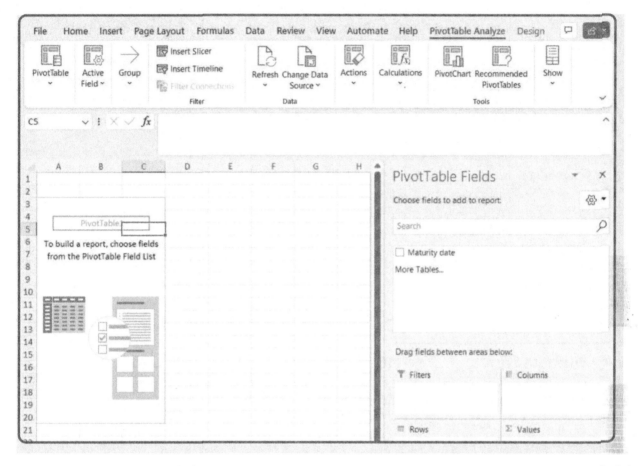

To access these options, simply click the black arrow on the right side of the values field and select **Value Field Settings**. This opens a dialog box where you can choose to sum, average, count, or even find the product of your data. Excel provides various summarization methods and display options, allowing for customized data presentation.

You can also apply custom calculations like percentages or running totals. After setting up these calculations, the Pivot Table can be formatted in the workspace to resemble a typical spreadsheet, making it more visually appealing and easier to read.

This feature transforms Pivot Tables from simple data summaries into comprehensive analytical tools, enabling users to extract more meaningful insights and present data in the most relevant way for their needs.

Keyboard Shortcuts on Excel

FUNCTION	PC SHORTCUT	MAC SHORTCUT
Undo action	Ctrl + Z	Command + Z
Center align cell contents	Alt + H, A, C	Command + E
Edit cell	F2	F2
Lock formula	F4	F4
Add line or column	Ctrl + +	Command + +
Delete line or column	Ctrl + -	Command + -
Hide selected row	Ctrl + 9	Command + (
Hide selected column	Ctrl + 0	Command +)
Go to formula tab	Alt + M	Command + Shift + U
Move cells in worksheet	Arrow keys	Arrow keys
Move to beginning of sheet	Ctrl + home	Command + home
Zoom in	Ctrl + Alt + =	Not available
Zoom out	Ctrl + Alt + -	Not available
Extend selection	Ctrl + Shift + Down arrow	Shift + Command + down arrow
Fill selected range with current entry	Ctrl + Enter	Command + return
Repeat last command	Ctrl + Y	Command + Y
Display function arguments	Ctrl + A	Command + A
Refresh data	Ctrl + F5	Command + F5

Chapter 3:
Microsoft PowerPoint

In today's professional world, creating presentations is often a daily task. While numerous tools exist for this purpose, **Microsoft PowerPoint** remains the preferred choice for many users. Whether for business or personal use, PowerPoint continues to offer the most comprehensive set of features for crafting effective presentations.

This chapter will explore the software's key functionalities and their practical applications. It's worth noting that PowerPoint shares some formatting and insertion tools with Excel and Word. For any questions about these shared features, readers can refer to the first two chapters of this book, which cover those applications in detail. PowerPoint's enduring popularity stems from its versatility and robust toolkit, making it an essential skill for many in the modern workplace.

Creating a Power Point Presentation

When you launch a new PowerPoint file, you're greeted with a **blank slide** featuring spaces for a title and subtitle. This forms the foundation of your presentation, which you'll customize with various elements like images and text. The initial interface is straightforward: a central slide view and a left-side scrollbar displaying all your presentation slides.

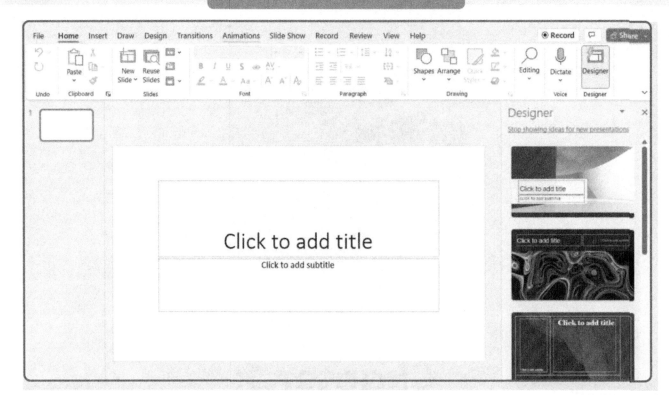

Home Tab

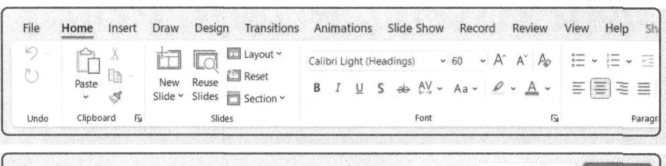

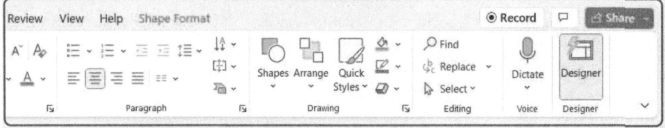

To **add new slides**, you have multiple options:

1. Use the "New Slide" button in the **Home tab's Slides section**
2. Click "New Slide" in the **Insert tab**
3. Right-click the **slide thumbnail panel** and select "New Slide"

New slides come with a default layout for titles and text. **Customize text using the Home tab's formatting tools**.

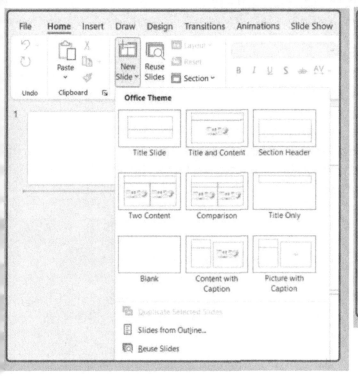

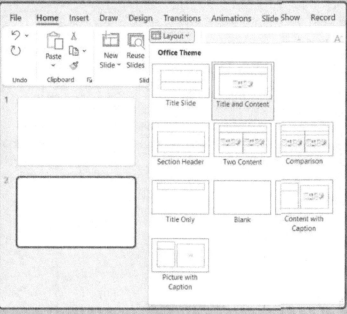

Changing slide layouts is simple:

1. Click the "Layout" button in the **Home tab's Slides section**
2. Right-click the slide and choose "Layout"

With an applied style, PowerPoint offers various layout options. Without a style, you'll see different content boxes to format as desired.

> **Pro tip:** *To insert a slide mid-presentation, click between slides in the thumbnail panel. A red line will appear, indicating the insertion point. Right-click and select "New Slide" to add it there.*

PowerPoint's flexibility allows you to craft presentations tailored to your needs, whether for business or personal use. Its intuitive interface and diverse tools make it a **powerful choice for creating engaging visual content**.

Managing Slides in PowerPoint

PowerPoint's intuitive design makes **slide organization and manipulation** straightforward, primarily through the **thumbnail panel** located on the left side of your screen. This panel offers a comprehensive overview of your presentation's structure and flow.

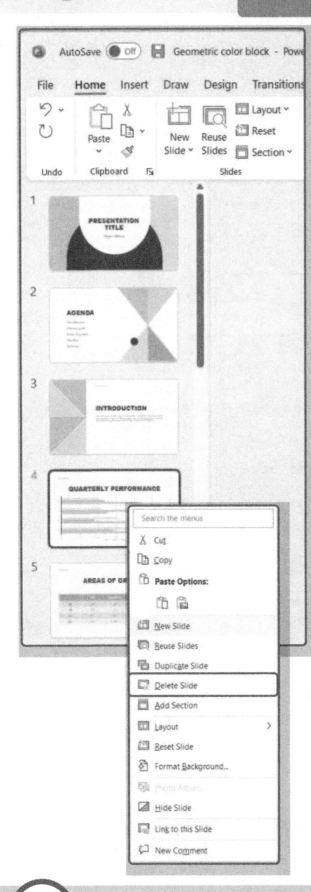

Navigating the Thumbnail Panel: The thumbnail panel is designed for easy navigation. It scrolls vertically, allowing you to view all slides in your presentation, regardless of length. Each thumbnail provides a miniature preview of the slide's content, making it easy to identify specific slides at a glance.

Rearranging Slides : To **reorder your presentation**, simply use the **drag-and-drop method** within the thumbnail panel:

1. Click and hold the slide you want to move.

2. Drag it to the desired position.

3. A horizontal line will appear between slides, indicating where the moved slide will be placed.

4. Release the mouse button to drop the slide into its new position.

Deleting Slides: There are multiple ways to **remove unwanted slides**:

1. Right-click the slide in the thumbnail panel and select "Delete Slide" from the context menu.

2. Select the slide in the thumbnail panel and press the Delete key on your keyboard.

3. Use the "Delete Slide" button in the Home tab of the ribbon, if available.

Recovering Deleted Slides If you accidentally delete a slide, don't panic. PowerPoint offers easy recovery options:

1. Use the **Undo function** (Ctrl+Z on Windows, Command+Z on Mac) immediately after deletion.

2. Click the Undo button in the Quick Access Toolbar at the top of the PowerPoint window

Working with Slide Layouts: PowerPoint templates often include **dotted lines** or place-holders on slides. These elements are crucial for slide design:

- They define content areas for text, images, and other elements.
- These lines and placeholders are not visible in the final presentation or slideshow mode.
- You can adjust these areas by clicking and dragging the borders of the placeholders.

Adding Text Boxes To add custom text areas:

1. Go to the **Insert tab** on the ribbon.
2. Click the **"Text Box" button** in the Text section.
3. Click and drag on your slide to draw the text box.
4. Start typing to add your content.

Insert Tab

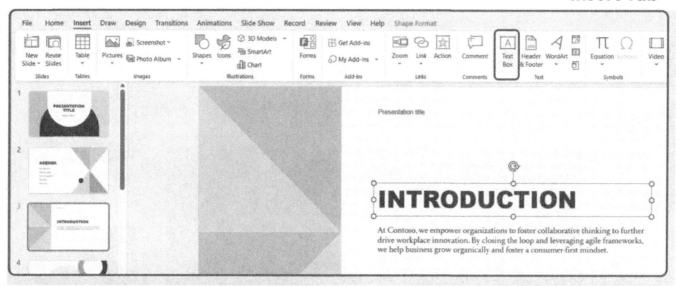

Pro Tips for Efficient Slide Management

1. Use the **Slide Sorter view** (found in the View tab) for a broader overview when reorganizing many slides.
2. Utilize **Sections** (Add Section in the Home tab) to group related slides together, especially in longer presentations.
3. Take advantage of **Duplicate Slide** (right-click a slide and select "Duplicate Slide") to create variations of a slide without starting from scratch.
4. Use **Hide Slide** (right-click and select "Hide Slide") to keep a slide in your presentation file without showing it during the presentation.

Applying Themes and Templates

PowerPoint offers a solution for those without company-provided presentation templates. Users can easily leverage themes and templates built into the software. These features serve different purposes: themes provide consistent color schemes and fonts across slides, while templates offer pre-designed layouts with placeholder content.

Themes are ideal for quickly refreshing existing presentations or maintaining visual consistency. **Templates** work best when starting from scratch and needing guidance on structure and layout. Understanding the distinction between these options helps users select the most appropriate tool for their needs. Whether you're creating a business proposal or an educational presentation, PowerPoint's themes and templates can elevate your content's visual appeal and professionalism. As you explore these features, you'll discover how to effectively enhance your presentations and captivate your audience.

Design Tab

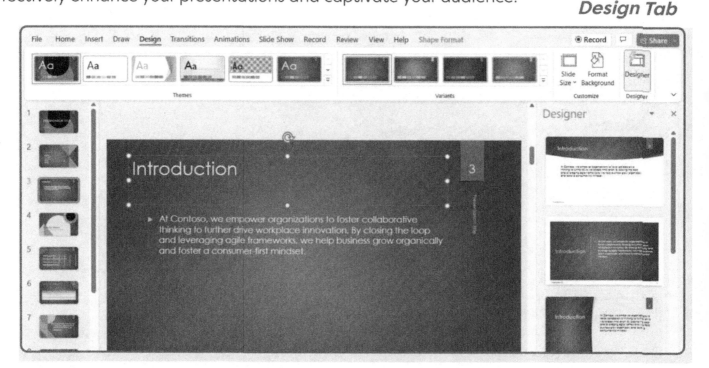

Themes

When creating a presentation in PowerPoint, you can enhance its visual appeal by applying a **theme**. Themes provide a cohesive look to your slides by automatically setting: Fonts, Colors, Styles and Visual effects.

Accessing Themes - To find and apply themes:

1. Go to the ribbon's **design tab**
2. Look under the **themes** section

3. Browse through standard presentation styles and their variations

Finding More Themes - PowerPoint offers built-in options, but you can expand your choices:

1. Click the down arrow on the right side of the theme box
2. Select **"Browse for Themes"** to search online for additional options

Consistency in Formatting - As you add new slides to your presentation:

- The chosen theme's formatting remains consistent
- This ensures a professional and uniform look throughout

Changing Layouts Within a Theme - If you want to change a slide's layout:

1. Use the "New Slide" function
2. PowerPoint will present pre-formatted layout options that match your theme
3. Choose the layout that best fits your content needs

Templates

PowerPoint templates can be accessed through the **File tab**. The software presents various **design options**, including the ability to select templates from online sources.

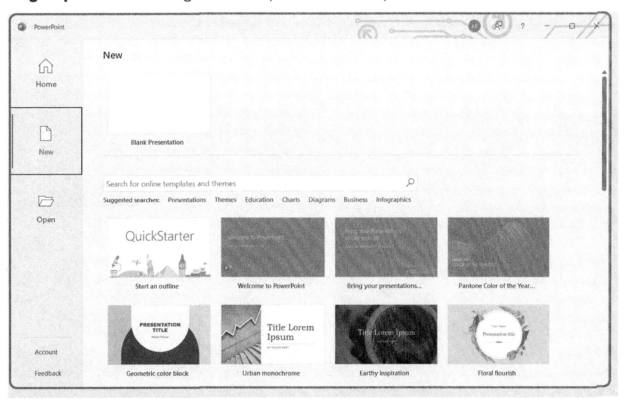

It's important to note that these templates are primarily focused on visual aesthetics rather than specific content needs. While some **themes** offer over 20 **slide layouts**, others may have fewer choices. Many templates come with a **predefined structure** for your presentation. However, users have the flexibility to **customize** these templates to better suit their specific requirements and preferences.

Creating a Master Presentation

Imagine you've been tasked by your company to create a **standard template** for everyone to use, or perhaps you want to design one for your own business or school. PowerPoint offers this capability through its **master slide** feature. Remember how templates or styles automatically set up new slides for you? That's the master slide feature at work.

You can create a **custom template** for your organization that includes: Company logo, Specific fonts, Color schemes, Chart styles, Image placeholders.

To access the master view:

1. Navigate to the **View tab** on the ribbon
2. Click on the **Slide Master** button within the **Master Views** section

Once you do this, the ribbon will change, displaying features exclusively related to master slides.

View Tab

In this view, you can:

- Design the **opening slide**
- Prepare different **layouts** for subsequent slides
- Add **page numbers** and **dates**
- Incorporate specific **themes** from the PowerPoint library

It's important to note that while in master view, all ribbon options pertain to master slides. To return to your regular presentation view, go to the **Slide Master tab** and click the **Close Master View** button.

Slide Master Tab

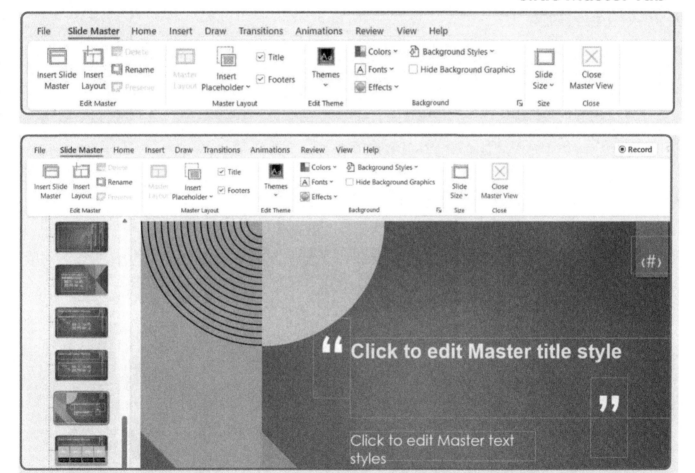

Pro tip: *After styling your master view, every new addition to your presentation will follow this template. This includes layouts, fonts, and overall appearance. You have the option to start a master template from scratch or modify an existing one, depending on your preferences.*

Empowering Your Slides: Pictures, Videos and Charts

PowerPoint allows users to enhance their presentations with various visual elements. These include pictures, icons, and videos, which can be used to illustrate key points. In newer versions of PowerPoint, most slide layouts offer quick access to insert different types of media. The options typically include tables, graphs, shapes, 3D objects, pictures (both local and online), and icons. These features enable users to create more dynamic and interactive presentations.

Inserting Pictures

Adding **images** to your PowerPoint presentation can be accomplished through various methods. The simplest approaches include:

- Using **copy and paste** functions
- Utilizing **keyboard shortcuts**
- Accessing options in the **ribbon interface**

When inserting a picture, PowerPoint offers the flexibility to choose files from your **local computer** or **online sources**. This process is similar for adding **shapes** or **SmartArt** elements. Initially, these visual elements will be placed within the slide's **work area**.

To adjust their size:

- Expand the work area
- Click and drag the image
- Hold the **Shift key** while resizing to maintain proportions

PowerPoint also provides an advanced feature called **Photo Album**. This tool is particularly useful when you need to showcase multiple images on a single slide without displaying them all simultaneously. To access this feature:

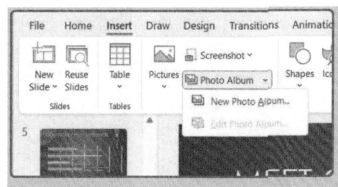

1. Navigate to the **Insert tab**
2. Locate the **Images section**
3. Click on the **Photo Album** button

Upon selecting this option, a **dialog box** will appear, allowing you to:

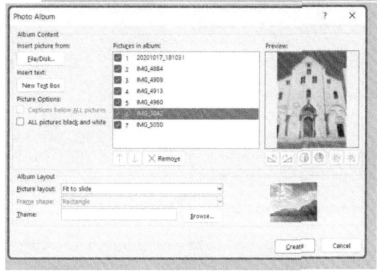

- Choose pictures from your computer
- Determine how images fit the slide
- Add captions if desired
- Select the album's shape or layout

To locate and add images to your album:

1. Use the **File/Disk** option in the dialog box

2. Browse and select desired images from your computer storage

The number of images you can add is flexible, depending on your presentation's intended size and structure. Once your album is created and added to the selected slide, you can navigate through the pictures during your presentation by:

- Clicking on the album
- Pressing the **Enter key**

By leveraging these image features, you can craft presentations that are not only informative but also visually appealing and memorable.

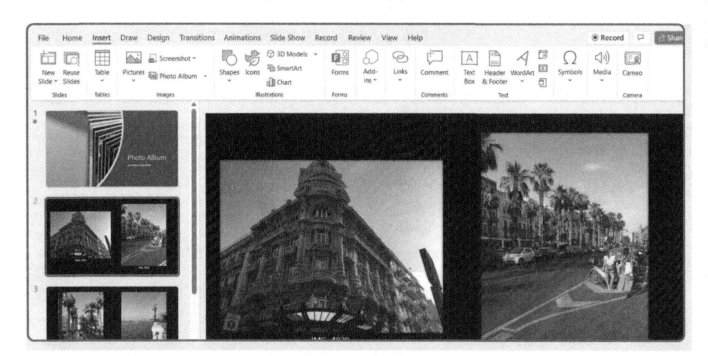

Adding Videos and Sound in Power Point

In the modern era of digital presentations, incorporating **multimedia elements** such as videos and audio can significantly elevate the quality and impact of your PowerPoint slides. These dynamic features not only engage your audience but also help convey complex information more effectively. Let's dive deep into the process of adding these elements to your presentations.

Adding Videos to Your Presentation

Videos can bring life to your slides, demonstrating concepts that might be difficult to explain with static images or text alone. PowerPoint offers two primary methods for incorporating videos:

1. **Online Videos :**These are sourced directly from the internet without downloading. Saves storage space on your device. Requires an internet connection during presentation

2. **Local Videos** : These are stored on your computer's hard drive. Can be played without internet access. Useful for custom or proprietary content

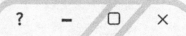

Insert Tab

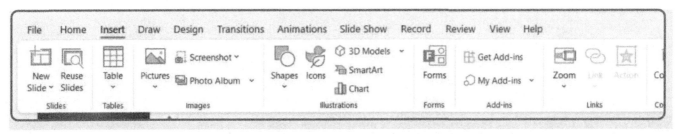

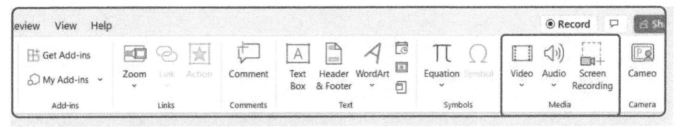

Step-by-Step Guide to Inserting Videos:

1. Open your PowerPoint presentation
2. Navigate to the **Insert tab** on the ribbon
3. In the **Media section**, click on the **Insert Video** dropdown arrow
4. Choose your video source for **Online Videos:**

   - Select **"Online Video"**
   - A dialog box will appear with supported platforms: YouTube, Vimeo, SlideShare, Stream, Flip
   - In your web browser, find the desired video on one of these platforms
   - Copy the video's URL from the address bar
   - Paste this URL into the PowerPoint dialog box
   - Click "Insert" to add the video to your slide

Online Videos

5. For **Local Videos:**

- Select **"This Device"**
- Browse your computer's files
- Select the desired video file
- Click **"Insert"**

Customizing Video Playback: Once your video is inserted, you can customize its appearance and behavior.

- Click on the video to reveal the **Video Tools** contextual tabs
- Use these tools to:
- Trim the video length
- Add a poster frame (static image displayed before play)
- Set playback options (auto-play, loop, etc.)
- Apply visual styles or effects
- Adjust size and position on the slide

Adding Sound to Your Presentation

Audio can complement your visuals and narration, adding depth to your presentation. PowerPoint allows you to add pre-recorded audio or record directly within the application.

Types of Audio in PowerPoint:

1. **Pre-recorded Audio Files**: Music tracks - Sound effects - Narrations recorded externally.

2. **Live Recordings**: Record your voice directly in PowerPoint - Useful for adding narration or explanations.

Steps to Insert Audio:

1. Go to the **Insert tab**
2. In the **Media section**, click on **Audio**
3. Choose your audio source:
4. For pre-recorded audio:

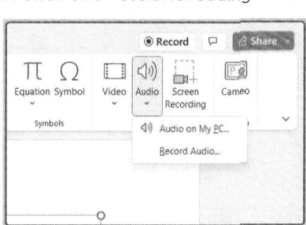

- Select **"Audio on My PC"**
- Browse and select your audio file
- Click "Insert" For recording audio:
- Select **"Record Audio"**
- Ensure your microphone is connected and recognized
- Click the red record button and speak
- Click stop when finished
- Name your recording and click **"OK"**.

Audio Playback Options: After inserting audio, you can customize its playback:

- Click on the audio icon to reveal **Audio Tools**
- Use these tools to:
- Trim the audio length
- Set volume levels
- Choose playback options (auto-play, hide icon, play across slides)
- Add fade-in or fade-out effects

Inserting Charts and Graphs in Power Point

The process of inserting charts and graphs in PowerPoint is straightforward and similar to the method used in Microsoft Word. Here's a detailed breakdown of the steps:

1. **Selecting Your Chart:**

- Navigate to the slide where you want to add the chart
- Click on the **Insert** tab in the ribbon
- Look for the **Charts** section and click on the **Chart** icon
- Choose from a variety of chart types (e.g., bar, line, pie, scatter)

2. Inputting Data:

- After selecting your chart type, PowerPoint will open an **Excel spreadsheet**
- This spreadsheet is where you'll enter your data
- As you input numbers, the chart in your PowerPoint slide will automatically update

3. Customizing Your Chart:

- Once your data is entered, close the Excel window

- Your chart will now appear on your PowerPoint slide

- You can further customize it using PowerPoint's built-in tools for formatting, colors, and styles

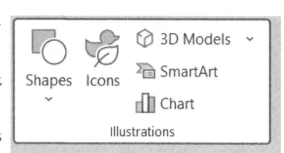

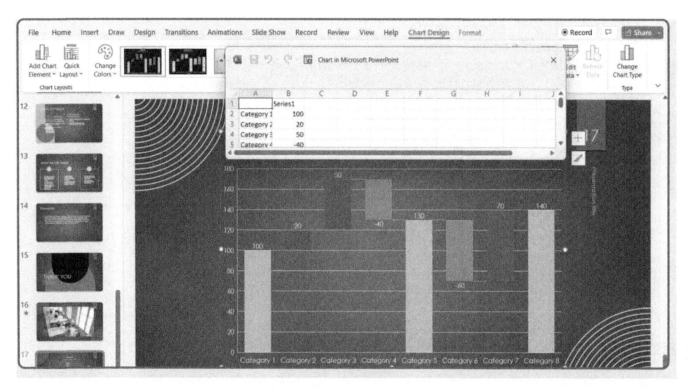

Importing Existing Charts from Excel

If you already have a chart created in Excel, you can easily transfer it to your PowerPoint presentation:

1. Copy and Paste Method:

- Open your Excel file containing the chart

- Select and copy the chart
- Switch to PowerPoint and paste it onto your desired slide

2. **Paste Options:** When you paste a chart from Excel, PowerPoint offers several **paste options**:

  - **Picture:** The chart becomes a static image
  - **Linked Chart:** Maintains a connection to the original Excel file
  - **Embed Chart:** Incorporates the chart data into PowerPoint

By mastering the art of incorporating charts and graphs into your PowerPoint presentations, you can significantly enhance your ability to communicate complex data effectively. Whether you're creating charts from scratch or importing existing ones from Excel, these visual elements can transform your slides from mere information carriers to powerful tools for insight and persuasion.

Animating and Transitioning a Presentation

Special effects in presentations can enhance audience engagement. These interactive elements come in two main forms:

1. **Transitions:** Animations that occur when moving between slides
2. **Animations:** Effects applied to individual elements within a slide

These features allow presenters to create more **dynamic and interactive presentations**, making complex information more digestible and maintaining audience interest throughout the delivery.

Transitions Tab

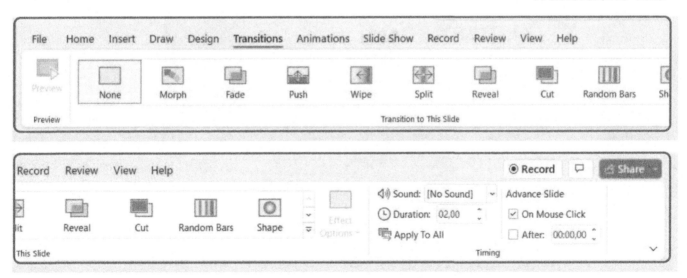

Inserting Transitions

Accessing Transitions

1. Open your **PowerPoint presentation**

2. Navigate to the **Transitions tab** on the ribbon. This tab is dedicated to all transition-related features

Selecting Slides for Transitions: Before applying a transition choose the slide you want to apply the transition to. You can select a slide in two ways:

1. Click on the slide in the main workspace
2. Select the slide thumbnail in the left-hand panel

Note: The transition you apply will affect how the slide enters, not how it exits.

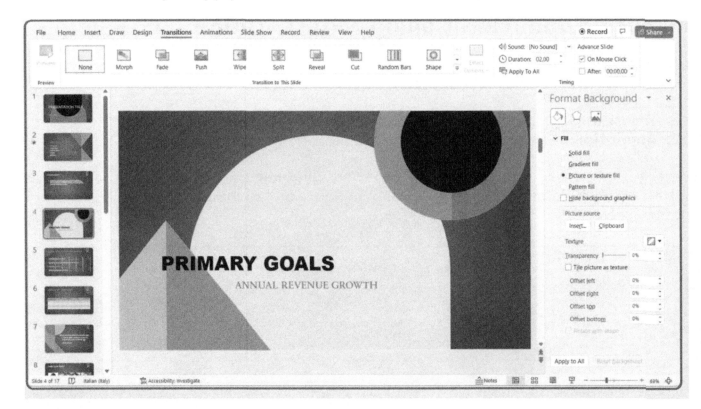

Choosing a Transition Effect

1. In the Transitions tab, you'll see a gallery of transition effects
2. These are grouped into three categories: • Subtle • Exciting • Dynamic Content
3. Click on any effect to apply it to your selected slide
4. Use the **More** arrow to see additional options

Previewing Transitions

- After selecting a transition, PowerPoint will automatically preview it once
- To see it again, click the **Preview** button on the far left of the **Transitions tab**
- This allows you to ensure the transition looks as intended

Preview

Preview

Customizing Transition Effects: Many transitions have additional options:

1. Look for the **Effect Options** button next to the transitions gallery
2. Click it to see variations of the selected transition
3. Experiment with these to fine-tune your transition's appearance

Removing Transitions

- Select the slide(s)
- In the Transitions tab, choose "None" from the transition gallery

<u>Inserting Animations</u>

Adding animations to individual elements in your PowerPoint slides is similar to applying transitions, but with more granular control. This feature allows you to **reveal information gradually**, keeping your audience focused.

Animations Tab

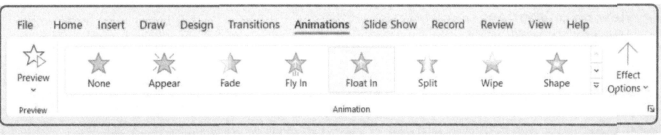

To insert animations:

1. Go to the **Animations tab** in the ribbon
2. Select the element you want to animate
3. Choose an animation type
4. Set the **duration and trigger** (e.g., mouse click or timed)

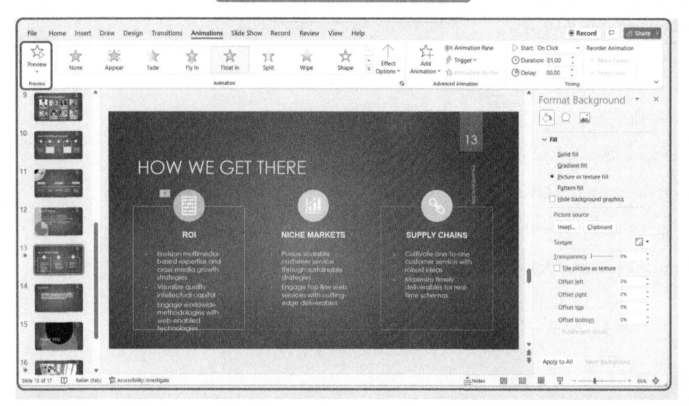

The **Animation Pane**, accessible from the Animations tab, is a powerful tool for managing multiple animations on a single slide. It appears on the right side of your workspace and allows you to:

- **View all animations** on the current slide
- **Adjust the order** of animations
- Set whether animations play automatically or require a trigger
- Modify animation duration
- **Preview the entire sequence**

You can also use the **Preview button** on the left side of the ribbon to see how your animations will look in the final presentation.

This level of control helps you create more engaging and dynamic slides, presenting information in a way that keeps your audience attentive and focused on your key points.

Comments and Notes

Adding supplementary information to your PowerPoint slides can be done in two ways notes and comments.

Speaker Notes:

1. These are **private reminders** for the presenter
2. To add notes, click the **"Click to add notes"** box below the slide
3. Notes are **visible only to you** during the presentation
4. They help you **remember key talking points**

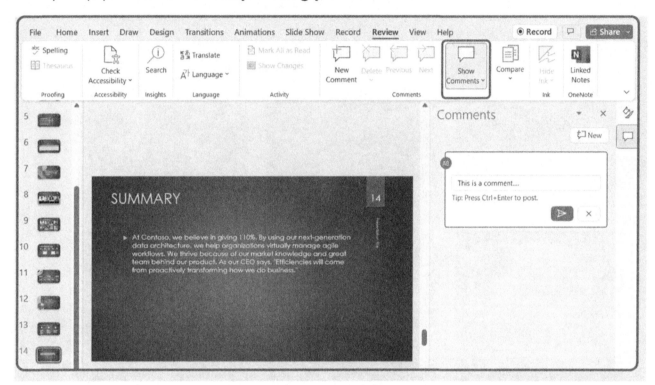

Comments: If you send this presentation to another person, you can also add a **comment** to the slide to include information that was not included in the file.

Comments are useful for **collaborative feedback.** To insert a comment:

1. Go to the **Review tab** in the ribbon
2. Click the **"Add Comment"** button

To view all comments:

1. Select the **"Show Comments"** option
2. Comments will appear with their associated slides. *Note: Comments are not visible during the actual presentation*

Both features **enhance the preparation process**, allowing for better organization of ideas and smoother collaboration.

Presentation and Print

PowerPoint offers several viewing options to help you visualize and finalize your presentation. These options are located near the zoom bar in the bottom right corner of your screen:

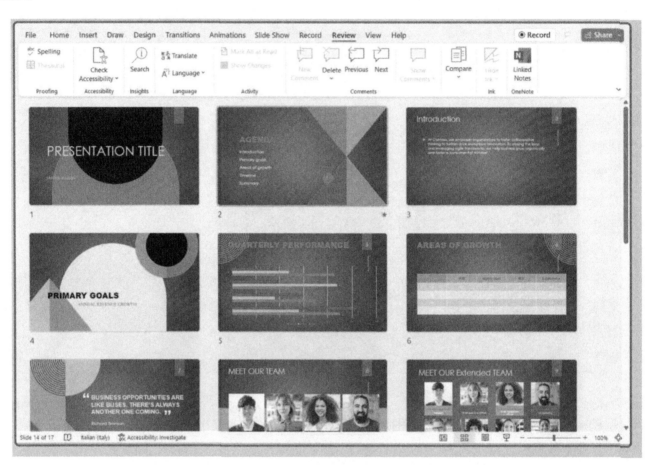

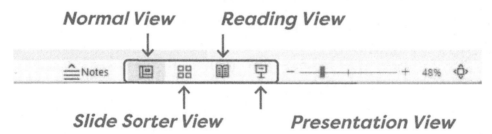

1. Normal View:

- The default view for editing and creating slides
- **Best for detailed work** on individual slides

2. Slide Sorter View:

- Displays thumbnails of all slides
- Allows you to **easily rearrange slide order**
- Doesn't allow content editing

3. Reading View:

- Shows how your presentation will look to the audience
- **Simulates the viewer's experience**

4. Presentation View: The most crucial view for presenters

- Displays:
  - A minimized version of the current slide
  - A preview of the next slide
  - Your speaker notes
- Most useful when presenting from your own device

Printing

PowerPoint offers **versatile printing options** to suit various needs. To access these, navigate to the **File tab** and select the **print function**. Here, you can customize how your presentation appears on paper. For a professional look, you might opt to **print one slide per page**, ideal for client presentations or course materials.

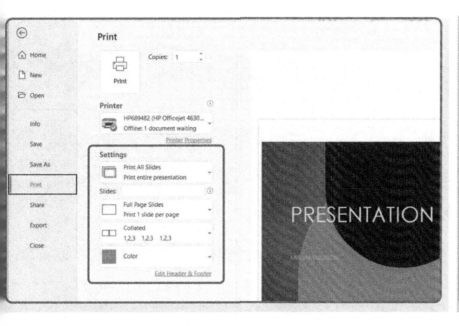

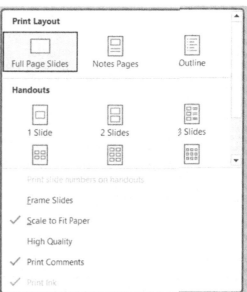

The **notes pages option** prints a slide at the top with space below for handwritten notes, perfect for speakers. If you only need an overview, the **outline option** prints just the headings and titles.

To conserve paper, you can **print multiple slides per page**, with PowerPoint allowing up to **nine slides on a single sheet**.

You can also adjust the **orientation** and choose between **single or double-sided printing** in the settings. These **flexible printing options** ensure you can **tailor the physical copy** of your presentation to your specific requirements.

Recording a Presentation

PowerPoint's **recording feature** is a powerful tool for creating automated presentations. This feature is particularly useful for **teachers**, **online course creators**, or anyone needing to deliver **pre-recorded content**.

Record Tab

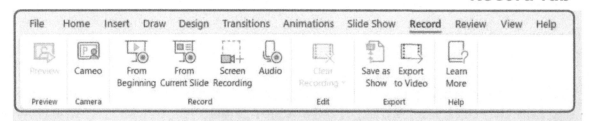

To access this tool, navigate to the **Record tab** in the ribbon. Here, you can choose to **start recording** from any selected slide or from the beginning of your presentation. After recording, you have the option to **add audio**, such as narration or background music.

Once you're satisfied with your recording, you can **export it as a video**. PowerPoint allows you to **save in various formats**, ensuring compatibility with your intended audience's devices or platforms.

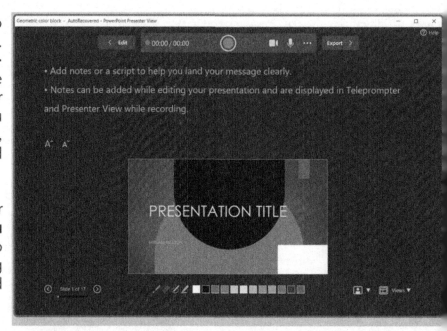

This **versatile recording function** transforms static slides into dynamic, narrated presentations, perfect for **distance learning**, **self-paced courses**, or **asynchronous communication** in professional settings.

Keyboard Shortcuts on Power Point

Function	PC Shortcut	Mac Shortcut
Start a presentation from the beginning	F5	Command + Shift + Return
Show presenter view	Alt + F5	Option + Return
Close presenter view	Esc	Esc
Move slide during presentation	Arrows or enter	Arrows or return
Go to last slide	End	End
Go to first slide	Home	Home
Go to next slide	Page down	Not available
Go to previous slide	Page up	Not available
Hide pointer and navigation	Ctrl + H	Not available
View computer taskbar	Ctrl + T	Not available
Add new slide	Ctrl + M	Command + Shift + N
Open Zoom dialogue box	Alt + W, Q	Command + (+) or (-)
Open recording feature	Alt + C	Not available
Expand or collapse the ribbon	Ctrl + F1	Command + F1
Select all objects in a slide	Ctrl + A	Command + A
Copy animation painter	Alt + Shift + C	Not available
Insert a text box	Alt + N, X	Not available
Insert WordArt	Alt + N, W	Not available
Group a selected group	Ctrl + G	Command + Option + G
Expand all groups	Alt + Shift + 9	Not available

Chapter 4:
Microsoft Access

Microsoft Access, despite being **underutilized** by many due to perceived complexity, stands as one of the most **powerful and versatile tools** in the Microsoft Office suite for creating and managing **information databases**. While the software allows users to build databases from the ground up, it also offers a wide array of **pre-designed templates** to jumpstart projects.

This **robust application** proves particularly valuable for **small to medium-sized businesses** that lack custom-built software solutions for their daily operational needs. Access provides a **cost-effective**, **scalable**, and **reliable system** for organizing and analyzing critical business data.

Core Functionality and User Interface

Access's interface is built around a **ribbon-based layout**, similar to other Microsoft Office applications, particularly Excel. This design choice significantly **reduces the learning curve** for users already familiar with the Office ecosystem. The similarity to Excel is especially beneficial for those proficient in **pivot table operations**, as many of these skills transfer seamlessly to Access's data manipulation capabilities.

The main sections of the Access ribbon include:

1. **Create tab**: Offers tools for building new database objects such as tables, queries, forms, and reports.

2. **External Data tab**: Provides options for importing, exporting, and linking data from various sources.

3. **Database Tools tab**: Contains utilities for database maintenance, analysis, and optimization.

While Access primarily focuses on **data management and analysis**, it doesn't neglect document aesthetics. The **Home tab** of the ribbon includes text formatting options similar to those found in Word and Excel. This feature allows users to create **polished, professional-looking reports and forms** that maintain consistency with other company documents.

Home Tab

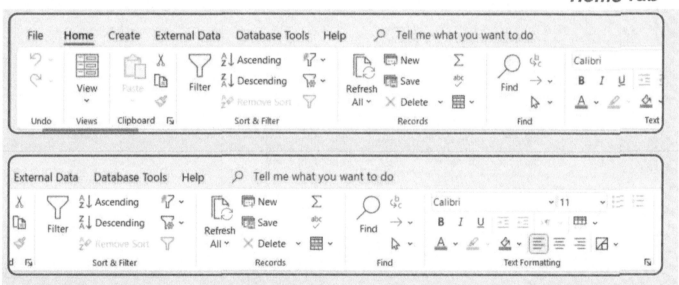

Advanced Features - For more experienced users, Access offers advanced capabilities:

- **Macros and VBA (Visual Basic for Applications)** for automation and custom functionality

- **Relational database design** to efficiently manage complex data structures

- **SQL view** for direct query writing and database manipulation

- **Integration with SharePoint** for improved collaboration and data sharing

- **Web database creation** for online access to database applications

Creating a New Database

Initiating a new database in Access follows a similar pattern to other Microsoft Office programs, accessible either upon launching the application or through the **File tab** in the ribbon. Users are presented with various options, ranging from a **blank database** for complete customization to **pre-formatted templates** provided by Microsoft.

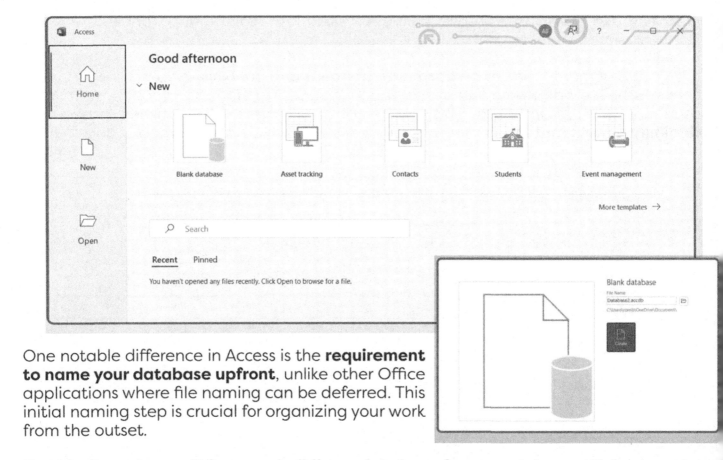

One notable difference in Access is the **requirement to name your database upfront**, unlike other Office applications where file naming can be deferred. This initial naming step is crucial for organizing your work from the outset.

For this discussion, we'll **focus on building a database from scratch**, as utilizing templates is relatively straightforward. When opting for a blank database, Access presents you with a **basic table structure** featuring unmarked rows and columns.

A key concept to grasp is Access's **dynamic row generation**. The software won't allow the addition of new rows until existing ones are populated. For example, once you complete the first row of data, Access automatically generates a second row for further input.

This approach encourages **structured data entry** and helps maintain database integrity from the start. It's a subtle yet powerful feature that guides users towards creating well-organized and coherent databases.

Customizing Field Names

The default blank database in Access comes with generic field names, which you'll likely need to **customize** to fit your specific data requirements. To rename these fields:

1. **Double-click** on the column header you wish to change.
2. The field name will become editable, allowing you to input a more appropriate title.

This **renaming process** applies not only to empty fields but also to those already containing data. To modify existing information:

3. **Double-click** on the cell you want to edit.
4. The cell content will be highlighted, making it ready for changes.

Key Insight: Access follows a structured approach to database expansion. You'll only be able to **add new columns** after naming the existing ones. Once you've labeled your current fields, Access will automatically provide the option to add more columns to your datasheet.

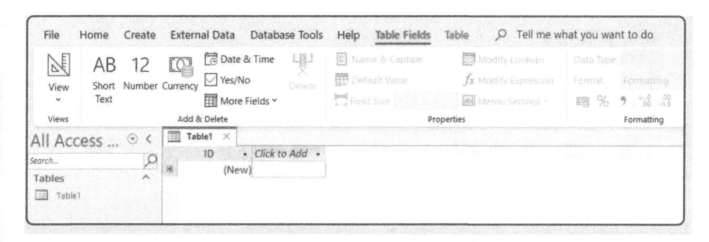

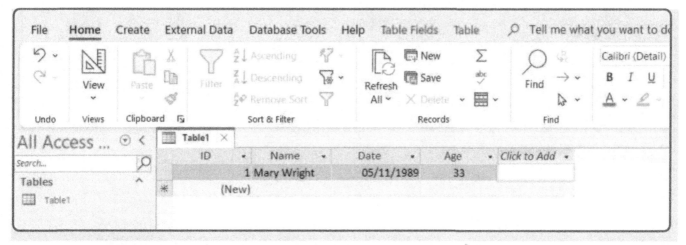

Pro tip: *When renaming fields, choose clear, descriptive names that accurately represent the data they'll contain. Avoid spaces in field names (use underscores if needed) and keep names concise yet informative. This naming convention will make your database more intuitive to use and easier to query in the future. Remember, well-structured field names form the foundation of a robust database, facilitating easier data entry, analysis, and reporting down the line.*

Data Organization: Filtering and Sorting

After populating your table with relevant data, Access immediately provides powerful tools for **data manipulation**:

Filtering Capabilities: Access allows you to **filter your information** based on various criteria. This feature helps you focus on specific subsets of your data, making analysis more manageable and targeted.

Sorting Options: You can easily **sort your data** in multiple ways:

- **Alphabetically**: Useful for text-based fields
- **Numerically**: For numerical data
- In both **ascending** or **descending** order

Home tab

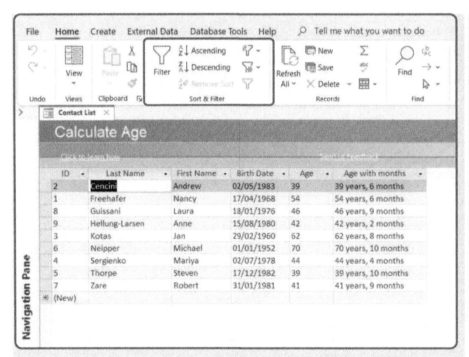

These sorting and filtering features in Access closely resemble those found in Excel, making them familiar to users with Excel experience. This similarity **enhances usability** across the Microsoft Office suite.

Data Visualization: While filtering and sorting can significantly improve data readability, Access offers additional tools for data presentation.

Reports: The report feature in Access provides a more **comprehensive view of your data**. It can automatically group and summarize information, offering insights that might not be immediately apparent in the raw table view.

> **Pro Tip:** *Experiment with different combinations of filters and sorts to uncover patterns or trends in your data. This exploratory approach can often lead to valuable insights that aren't obvious at first glance.*

Expanded Access Features

While primarily a data storage tool, Access offers additional functionalities:

- The **Create tab** in the ribbon provides options for adding media, dialogue boxes, check-boxes, and blank forms.

- **Application Parts** and **Blank Form** buttons allow for customized data input interfaces.

- These features enable structured data mapping and standardized input methods.

- Users can contribute data without accessing the entire database.

Access also includes familiar Microsoft Office tools:

- Spell check
- Equation editor
- Find and replace function

These operate consistently across the Microsoft Suite. For detailed usage, refer to earlier chapters on other Office applications.

Adding New Tables

Tables are the cornerstone of Microsoft Access, serving as the primary tool for data organization and storage. Understanding how to effectively manage tables is crucial for maximizing the potential of this powerful database software.

When you create a new table, Access automatically generates a tab labeled **"Table 2"** (or the next sequential number) at the top of your work area. This default naming can quickly become confusing as your database grows in complexity.

Create tab

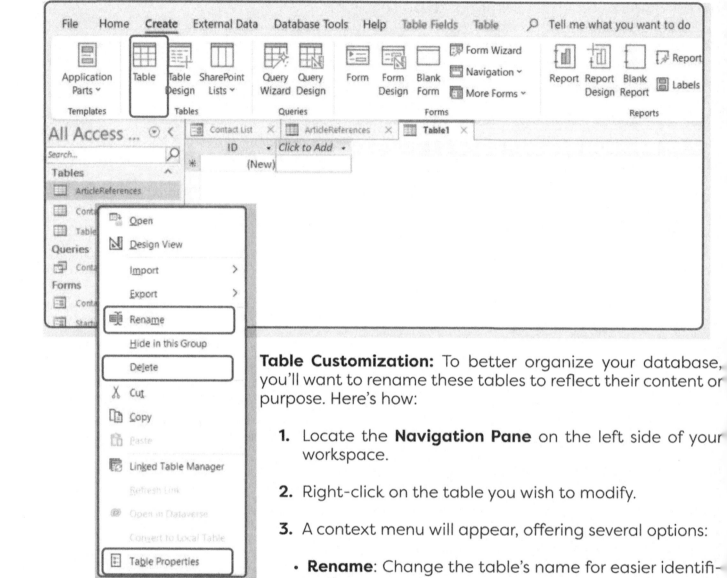

Table Customization: To better organize your database, you'll want to rename these tables to reflect their content or purpose. Here's how:

1. Locate the **Navigation Pane** on the left side of your workspace.

2. Right-click on the table you wish to modify.

3. A context menu will appear, offering several options:

   - **Rename**: Change the table's name for easier identification.
   - **Delete**: Remove the table entirely (use with caution).
   - **Properties**: View and modify the table's attributes.

Populating Your Tables: When working with a new table, you'll follow the same data entry process as with your initial table:

- **Add information row by row and column by column.**
- Access dynamically generates new rows as you complete existing ones.
- Consider each new table as a separate document that you can later link to other tables in your database.

Importing External Data

Access offers robust capabilities for integrating data from external sources, streamlining the process of building comprehensive databases.

Accessing Import Features:

1. Navigate to the **External Data** tab in the ribbon.
2. Click on the **New Data Source** button to begin the import process.

External Data tab

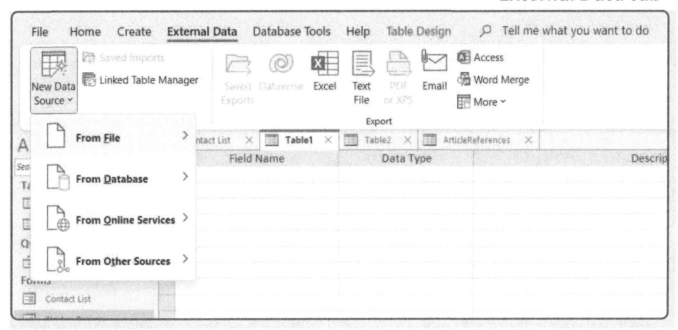

Data Source Options: Access provides flexibility in importing data from various locations:

- Files stored on your local computer
- Online sources
- Other databases
- Additional data repositories

Import Methods: Once you've selected your data source, Access presents three primary options for integrating the data:

1. **Import to a New Table**: Creates a fresh table with the imported data.

2. **Append to an Existing Table**: Adds the new data to a table you've already established.

3. **Link to Excel**: Maintains a dynamic connection between your Access database and an Excel spreadsheet.

Excel Linking Feature: When you choose to link to an Excel file, any modifications made to the original Excel document will automatically reflect in your Access database. This feature ensures your data remains up-to-date across platforms.

If the changes don't appear immediately, you can manually update by clicking the **Refresh** button located in the **Home** tab of the ribbon.

Efficient Workspace Management: As your database grows, you may find yourself working with multiple tables simultaneously. Access provides tools to help manage your workspace effectively.

Closing Table Views:

When you're not actively using a particular table, you can temporarily remove it from view:

- Click the **X** button on the table's tab to close it.
- This action doesn't delete the table; it simply removes it from your immediate work-space.

Reopening Tables:

To bring a closed table back into view:

- Locate the table name in the **Navigation Pane** on the left side of your screen.
- Click on the table name to reopen it in your workspace.

> *Pro Tip for Power Users: Efficiently managing your open tables can significantly improve your workflow in Access. Regularly close tables you're not actively using to reduce clutter and enhance focus on your current task. Remember, closing a table view doesn't affect the data within – it's always safely stored in your database, ready to be accessed when needed.*

Formatting Fields

One of Access's most powerful features is its intuitive field formatting capabilities. Unlike other database software that might require manual configuration, Access offers a range of quick tools to streamline the process of setting up your data fields.

Quick Field Formatting Options

With just a few clicks, you can define the data type for any column or field in your table. The most commonly used data types include:

1. **Short Text**: For brief alphanumeric entries
2. **Number**: For numerical data
3. **Currency**: For financial figures, automatically formatted with currency symbols
4. **Date and Time**: For temporal data, with various date and time format options
5. **Yes/No**: For binary data, often displayed as checkboxes

These options are readily available in the quick tools menu, allowing for rapid table setup.

If these standard options don't meet your specific needs, Access provides an extensive array of additional field types. By clicking the **More Fields** button (identified by a downward-pointing arrow), you'll access a comprehensive list of specialized field types.

Table Fields tab

Some noteworthy options include:

- **Address Fields**: Automatically creates a set of fields for storing complete address information (street, city, state, zip code, country)

- **Payment Type**: Generates a data validation menu with common payment methods

- **Status Bar**: Useful for project management, allowing you to track progress visually

These are just a few examples of the diverse field types available. By exploring the full range of options, you can tailor your database structure to precisely match your data management needs.

Best Practices for Field Addition

When adding new fields to your database using the quick formatting buttons, it's important to note that Access will not overwrite existing data. Instead, it adds the new fields to your table structure. To maintain the logical organization of your table:

End-of-Table Insertion: Always position your cursor in the last available column before adding new fields. This ensures that new fields are appended to the end of your table structure.

Strategic Placement: If you need to insert a new field in the middle of your existing structure, place your cursor in the column immediately before your desired insertion point.

Creating Calculated Fields

One of the most powerful yet often overlooked features in Microsoft Access is the ability to use **calculated fields**. This functionality brings the computational power of Excel spreadsheets directly into your Access database, allowing for dynamic data analysis and manipulation. To add a calculated field to your Access table:

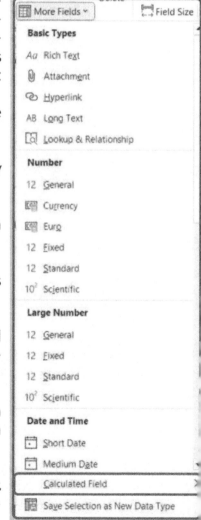

1. **Select the Column**: Click on the header of the column where you want to insert the calculated field.

2. **Access the Table Fields Tab**: This tab will automatically appear in the ribbon once you've selected a column.

3. **Locate More Fields**: Click on the **"More Fields"** button in the ribbon.

4. **Choose Calculated Field**: Near the bottom of the options list, you'll find **"Add Calculated Field."** Select this option.

Configuring Your Calculation: Upon selecting "Add Calculated Field," a dialog box will open, providing you with a canvas to design your calculation:

1. **Field Selection**: Choose the fields you want to include in your calculation. These will typically be other columns in your table.

2. **Formula Construction**: In the provided text box, construct your formula using the selected fields and appropriate operators.

Enter an Expression to calculate the value of the calculated column:
(Examples of expressions include [field1] + [field2] and [field1] < 5)

OK
Cancel
Help
<< Less

Expression Elements | Expression Categories | Expression Values
Table new Access | Field1 | <Value>
Functions | ID |
Constants |
Operators |

Example Calculation: Let's consider a practical example of a calculated field:

([Field 1] + [Field 2] + [Field 3]) / 3

This formula calculates the average of three specified fields. Once set up, Access will automatically compute this average for each record in your table, updating dynamically as the source data changes.

Pro Tip: Data Type Compatibility

When setting up calculated fields, pay close attention to the data types of the fields involved in your calculations. For instance:

1. ***Numerical Calculations:*** *Ensure all fields are number types (Integer, Double, etc.) for accurate mathematical operations.*
2. ***Date Calculations:*** *Use Date/Time fields for date-based computations.*
3. ***Text Manipulations:*** *String functions work best with Text field types.*

Mixing incompatible data types can lead to errors or unexpected results. Access will often try to convert data types automatically, but it's best practice to manage this explicitly for reliability and performance.

Advanced Field Management

Rearranging Fields with Drag and Drop: Microsoft Access offers a user-friendly approach to reorganizing your database structure through its drag and drop functionality. This feature allows you to easily reposition columns within your table view:

1. **Selecting a Field**: Click on the title of the column you wish to move.

2. **Visual Guide**: A black line will appear to the left of the selected column, serving as a visual indicator.

3. **Repositioning**: Drag the column to your desired location. The black line will show where the column will be placed upon release.

This intuitive method allows for quick and easy table reorganization to suit your specific needs or preferences.

> **Pro Tip: Column Width Customization** *Similar to Excel, Access allows manual adjustment of column widths and row heights. This feature enables you to optimize your table's visual layout for better readability and data presentation.*

Enhanced Field Management Options: Access provides a range of additional field management tools, easily accessible through a right-click context menu on any column header. This menu offers several powerful options:

1. **Copy and Paste**: Duplicate column content or structure.
2. **Hide/Unhide Fields**: Temporarily remove fields from view or bring them back.
3. **Insert Fields**: Add new columns at specific locations.
4. **Freeze Columns**: Lock specific columns in place for easier navigation.

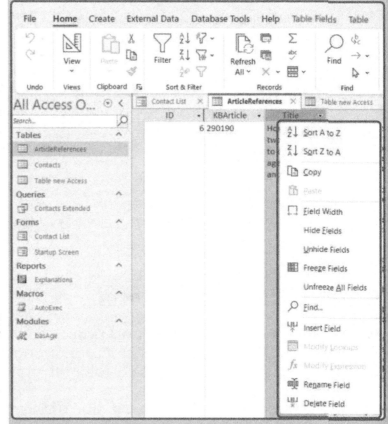

The Power of Freezing Fields: The 'Freeze' feature is particularly valuable when working with extensive databases that require horizontal scrolling.

Unlike Excel, which typically freezes everything to the left of a selected column, Access allows for more granular control:

- **Selective Freezing**: Freeze individual columns as needed.

- **Custom Order**: Frozen columns are arranged in the order they were frozen.

- **Easy Unfreezing**: Return to normal view with a single click.

Practical Application: Student Grade Database

Consider a scenario where you're managing a database of 9th-grade student grades:

- Each row represents a student.

- Each column represents a different class.
- You have 20+ columns of grade data.

To maintain context while scrolling through extensive grade data:

1. Right-click on the student name column.
2. Select **"Freeze Fields"** from the context menu.
3. The name column will move to the leftmost position and remain visible as you scroll horizontally through the grade data.

You can freeze additional columns (e.g., student ID, homeroom) in a similar manner. These will be positioned to the right of previously frozen columns.

Unfreezing and Restoring Original Layout

To revert to the original table view:

1. Right-click on any frozen column.
2. Select "Unfreeze All Fields" from the context menu.

Important Note: Unfreezing will release all frozen columns simultaneously. However, this action does not automatically restore the original column order. To reestablish the initial layout, you'll need to manually reposition the columns using the drag and drop method described earlier.

Relations and Queries

Relations and queries are fundamental tools in Access, setting it apart from Excel. These features enable rapid information retrieval, establish connections between database elements, and facilitate report generation. Let's explore their functions in detail.

Establishing Relations

To illustrate the significance of relations in Access, consider a database for managing student information and grades. Imagine you've created a table containing students' grades and now want to add a separate table for their personal information. **It's crucial to have at least one common field between these tables to establish a connection**.

This could be a unique student ID number or a combination of first and last names, depending on your preference. However, **creating a unique identifier for each student is generally the most effective approach**.

When setting up the new table for personal information, include relevant details such as addresses, phone numbers, teacher names, and any other pertinent data. The key is to ensure that the information uniquely identifies each student, facilitating easy retrieval and management.

1. **Create two tables:**

   - **Table 1:** Student grades
   - **Table 2:** Student personal information

2. Ensure at least **one field is common** between the tables:

   - **Option A:** Student ID number (recommended)
   - **Option B:** First and last names

Note: Using a unique ID is generally the best practice for easy identification.

3. Steps to **establish relationships:**

   - Navigate to the **database tools tab** in the ribbon
   - Click on the **relationships** button

Database Tools Tab

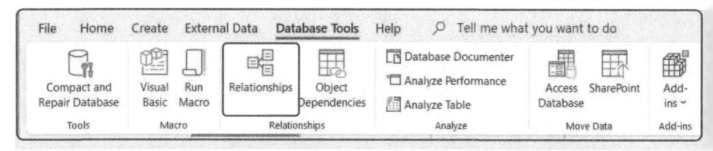

   - In the new workspace view, double-click table names to open them
   - Observe the **primary key** indicated by a key icon next to field names
   - Drag the relevant field from one table to the corresponding field in the other
   - Define the relationship type in the dialog box that appears

4. Finalizing the relationship:

   - Click the **"X"** on the relationship tab
   - Save and name the relationship when prompted
   - The named relationship will appear in the left-hand pane of the database view

After setting up the relationship, you have the option to name and save it. Upon saving Access will display the relationship in the left-hand pane of the database view, making it easily accessible for future use or modifications.

Relationships Design Tab

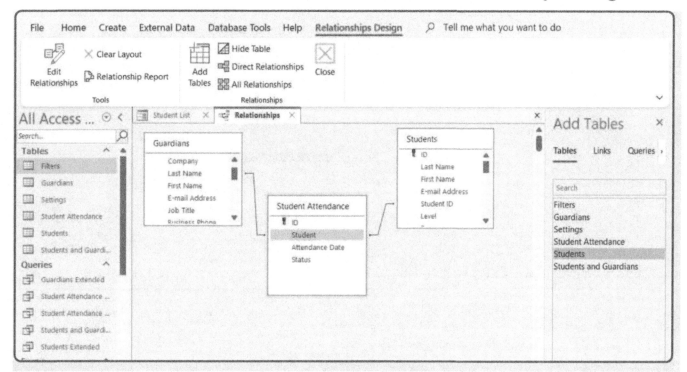

Queries

Queries are powerful tools in Access that allow you to filter and analyze your database information. They range from simple to complex, enabling you to visualize data according to specific needs. Here's a comprehensive guide to creating queries:

Create tab

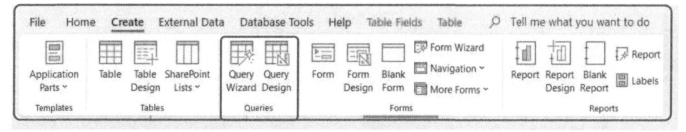

Creating a Query:

1. Navigate to the **create tab** in the ribbon
2. In the **queries section**, choose between:

   - Using the **wizard** for guided creation
   - Using **query design** for manual creation

Steps to Create a Custom Query:

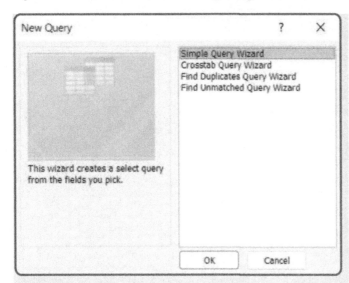

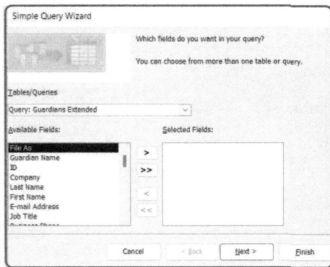

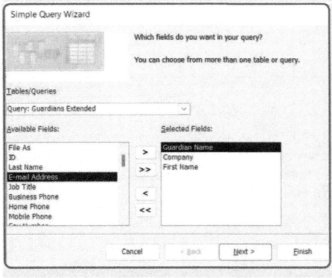

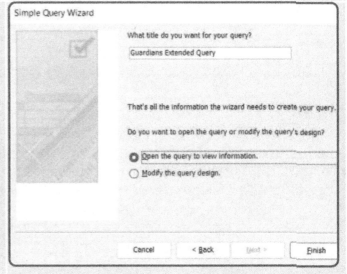

1. Click on the **new query** button
2. In the new workspace view:

   • Select relevant tables by double-clicking or drag-and-drop
   • Observe relationships between tables (e.g., **student ID number**)

3. Select fields for your query:

   • Double-click desired fields in table boxes
   • Fields appear in the table below the workspace

4. Set criteria for your query:

- Locate the column with the relevant information
- In the **criteria line**, enter your condition (e.g., "=>80%")

5. Save and name your query

Example Query: Students with Math Grades Below 80%

Fields to include:

- **Student ID**
- **Student Name**
- **Math Grade**

Criteria: In the Math Grade column, enter "<80%" in the criteria line

This query will display all students with math grades below 80%, allowing for quick identification of those needing additional support.

Types of Queries:

1. **Select Queries:** Retrieve specific data
2. **Filter Queries:** Narrow down data based on criteria
3. **Calculation Queries:** Perform mathematical operations on data
4. **Cross-tab Queries:** Summarize data in a matrix format
5. **Action Queries:** Make changes to data (update, delete, append)

Query

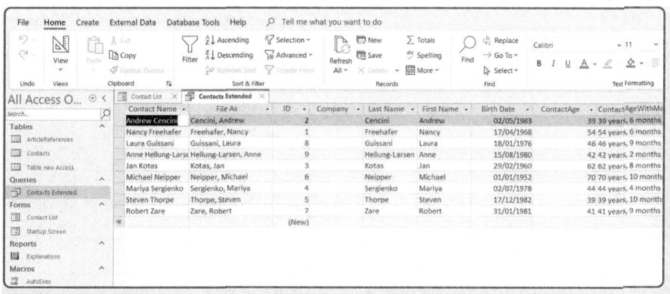

Creating Reports

Creating reports is the final crucial step in utilizing Access to its full potential. After establishing databases and relationships, generating reports allows you to present your information effectively. This process is relatively straightforward, as the groundwork has already been laid in previous steps. **Reports in Access offer dynamic features, including customizable styles**. You can choose from predetermined styles or create your own to suit your needs. For instance, if you're creating a student grade report card, you can include personal information, subjects, and grades in a visually appealing format.

To create a report, navigate to the **create tab** in the ribbon and select the **report** button. This action opens a new window and displays the **report design layout** toolbar in the ribbon. For those unsure about the report's final appearance, Access provides a **report wizard** to guide you through the process and help determine the best approach for your report.

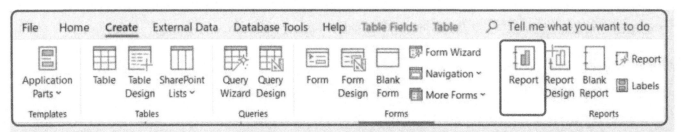

Report Layout Deisgn Tab

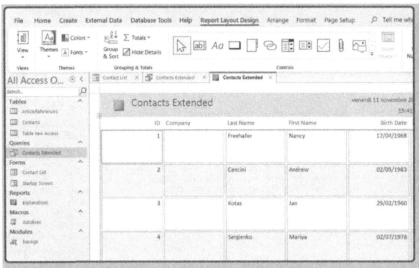

When designing your report, you can select the information you want to include based on your specific requirements. **You have the flexibility to add various elements such as logos, titles, page numbers, and images to enhance the report's visual appeal and functionality**.

After selecting all the necessary fields and customizing the layout, simply close the view by clicking the **x** button. Don't forget to save the report under your desired name. The newly created report will then appear in the left-hand pane of the program for easy access.

Pro tip: use the "print preview" option to ensure the report meets your expectations before finalizing it. This allows you to make any necessary adjustments and guarantees that the final product aligns with your vision.

Keyboard Shortcuts on Access

Function	PC Shortcut	Mac Shortcut
Go to home tab	Ctrl + H	Command + H
Open existing database	Ctrl + O	Command + O
Switch views of database	F5	Not available
Switch from edit to view mode	F2	Not available
Move to other datasheet view	Tab key or Shift + Tab	Tab key
Exit Access	Alt + F4	Not available
Go to create tab	Alt + C	Not available
Go to table tab	Alt + J, T	Not available
Go to database tools tab	Alt+Y, 2	Not available
Go to external data tab	Alt + X	Not available
Show or hide property sheet	F4	Not available
Move to beginning of entry	Home	Home
Move to end of entry	End	End
Move between lines	Arrow keys	Arrow keys
Move to next field	Tab key	Tab key
Move to previous field	Shift + Tab	Not available
Select a column	Shift + arrow key	Shift + arrow key
Remove the selected column	Spacebar or (-) sign	Not available

Chapter 5:
Microsoft Outlook

Email has become a dominant form of communication in today's world. To facilitate this, Microsoft includes a dedicated email application in its suite: Microsoft Outlook. Unlike other Microsoft applications, Outlook requires users to set up their accounts before use.

Account Setup

While there are multiple ways to configure an Outlook account, we'll focus on the most common method for personal email users with accounts on platforms like Gmail, Yahoo, or Hotmail. **The setup process differs slightly depending on whether you're using Outlook for the first time or not.** For first-time users, a welcome screen with instructions will appear. For existing users, you'll need to navigate to the account settings manually.

To begin, access the File tab in the ribbon and select Account Settings. In the dialog box that opens, go to the Email tab and click the New button (marked with a small envelope icon) to add your account. Enter your email address in the new window that appears, then click Connect. **You'll need to provide your name, email address, and password.** After clicking Next, you may be prompted to re-enter your password. Finally, click Finish to complete the setup.

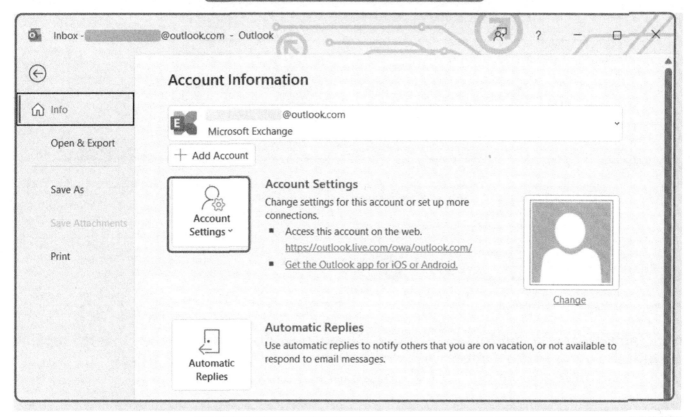

Once configured, you'll be directed to your Inbox, where you can manage your messages.

The Home tab in the ribbon provides access to most message-related features.

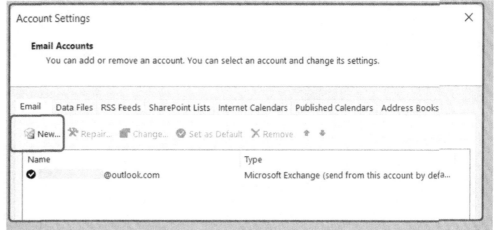

Outlook's ribbon is relatively straightforward, consisting of only four main tabs in addition to the Help and File tabs.

Setting a Signature

One of the first tasks many users want to accomplish in Outlook is creating a signature. To do this, start by opening a new message. You don't need to actually compose an email; this step just gives you access to the signature settings.

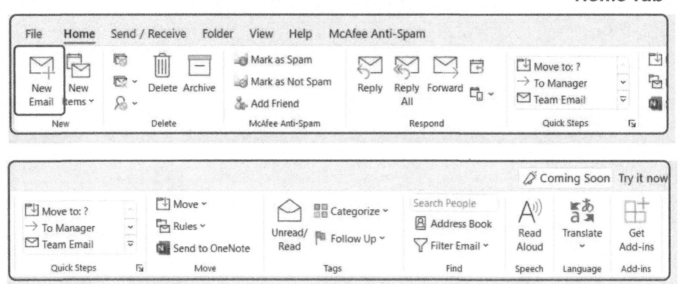

In the new message window, locate the "Signature" option under the "Insert" section of the Message tab in the ribbon. Click on this button and select **"Signatures"** to open a new dialog box where you'll input your signature information.

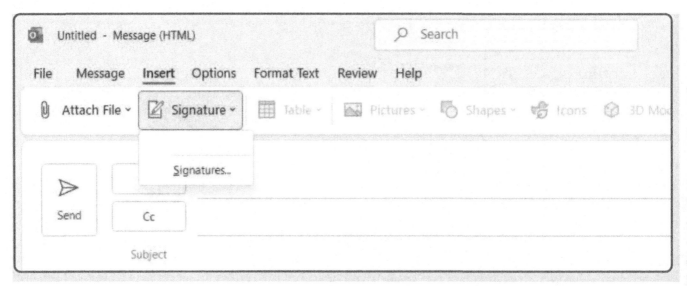

To create a new signature, click "New" and give it a name. This name will appear in a drop-down menu for easy selection when adding signatures manually. In the largest box at the bottom, labeled **"Edit signature,"** type the content you want to use as your email sign-off. You can customize the font, color, and other style elements similar to other Microsoft Suite applications.

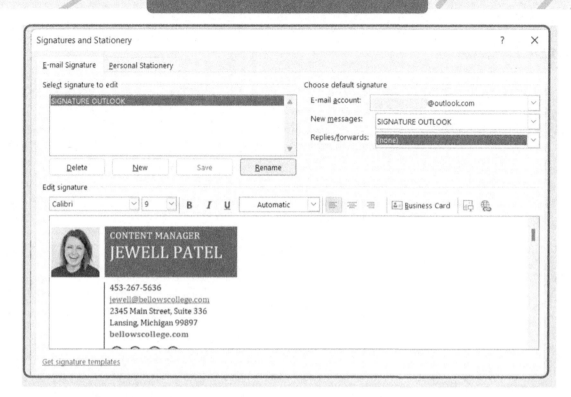

After creating your signature, you can specify when it should be used automatically. In the right-hand menu labeled **"Choose default signature,"** you can assign different signatures to different email accounts (if you have multiple). **You can set default signatures for new messages, replies, and forwards separately.**

If you prefer not to use automatic signatures, you can leave these fields blank and manually insert signatures as needed. In this case, set up your signature but don't configure the default options. When composing a message, you can then go back to the signature button and choose which signature to use for that specific email.

Sending Emails

To start a new email, simply click the "New Email" button. This opens a message box where you can type your content. While you can format your message using the text formatting tools in the ribbon, keep in mind that not all recipients may see the formatting exactly as you intended. The appearance can vary depending on the email program and settings used by the receiver.

The "To" and "Cc" (carbon copy) fields are readily visible, but the "Bcc" (blind carbon copy) field needs to be added manually.

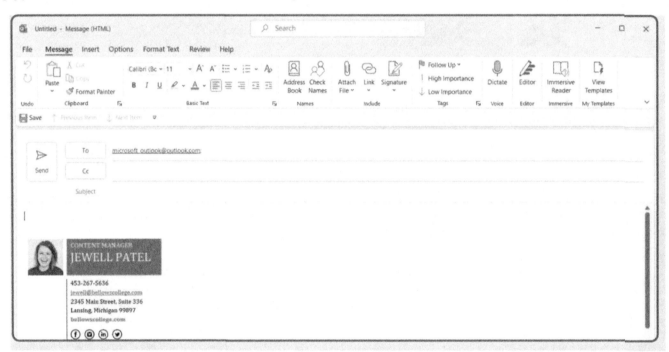

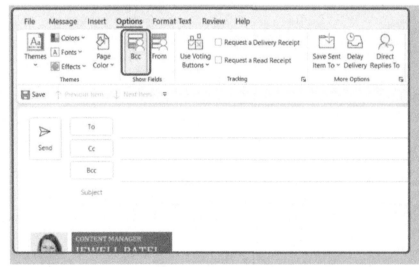

To do this, click on either the **"To"** or **"Cc"** buttons to open a dialog box that includes the **Bcc option.** Enter an address and click "OK" to continue.

Alternatively, you can expose the Bcc field by going to the Options tab in the ribbon. Under the "Show Fields" section, you'll find buttons for "Bcc" and "From."

Clicking these buttons will display the corresponding fields, allowing you to modify visible information as needed.

The Options tab also allows you to request read and delivery receipts from the recipient. You can check boxes to select whether you want to be notified when your message is received or read. **These settings can be applied to all your outgoing messages, meaning you'll get a notification each time a message is received or read.**

Delayed Delivery

Outlook allows you to schedule emails for future delivery, such as the next morning.

Options Tab

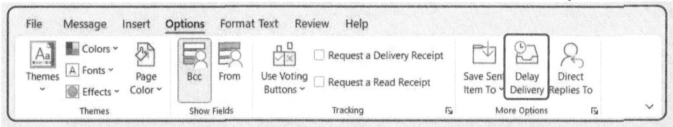

1. To access this feature, go to the **Options tab** and look for the **"More Options"** section.

2. Click on the **"Delay Delivery"** option to open a dialog box where you can set your preferences.

You can specify when you want the message delivered, designate who should receive replies, and set an expiration time for the message.

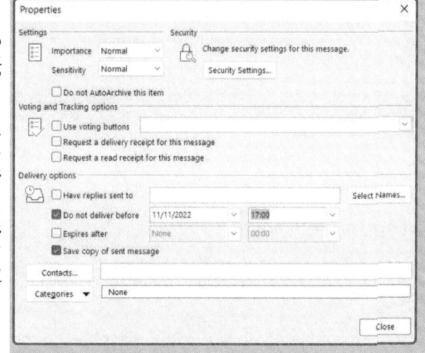

Determining Importance for each E-Mail

Outlook enables you to assign priority levels to your emails. You can mark a message as high priority by clicking the exclamation mark icon, or as low priority by clicking the blue downward-pointing arrow.

Message Tab

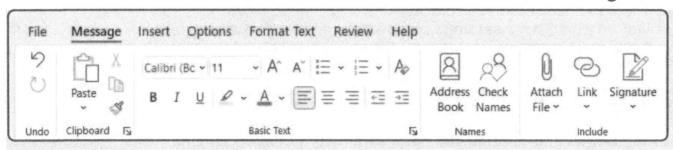

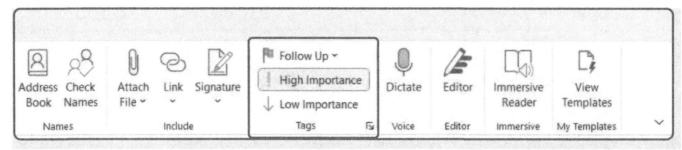

You can also flag messages for follow-up by clicking the red flag icon. This opens a drop-down menu where you can choose when you want to be reminded to follow up on the email.

While Outlook offers some standard reminder options, you can also set a custom reminder date to suit your needs.

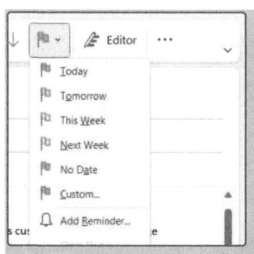

Polling Through Email

Outlook offers a built-in polling feature that can streamline group decision-making processes. This tool is particularly useful when you need approvals or opinions from multiple recipients.

To create a poll, navigate to the Options tab while composing your email. In the Tracking section, you'll find a button labeled **"Use Voting Buttons."** Clicking this button reveals a drop-down menu with pre-set voting options:

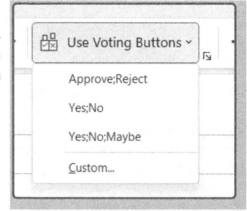

- Accept or Reject
- Yes, No, Maybe

These default options cover many common scenarios, but Outlook also allows for customization. If you need more specific voting choices, you can create your own. Simply select the "Custom" option in the drop-down menu, and a dialog box will appear. Here, you can enter your personalized voting options, separating each choice with a semicolon.

When recipients receive your email, they can easily cast their vote by clicking their preferred option. Outlook automatically collects and organizes these responses, making it simple for you to track the results.

This polling feature can significantly enhance collaboration and decision-making efficiency, especially for teams working remotely or across different time zones. It provides a quick and organized way to gather feedback or reach consensus on various matters, from scheduling meetings to approving project proposals.

Adding Attachments and Images

"**Images and pictures**" can be incorporated directly into the "**body of an email**" instead of being sent as attachments. However, it's important to realize that not all recipients may see these images inline; some might receive them as separate attachments depending on their email client settings.

To add images, use the "**ribbon features**" in your email composition window, which work similarly to those in other Microsoft applications we've discussed. When deciding how to include images, consider your audience and their potential technical limitations.

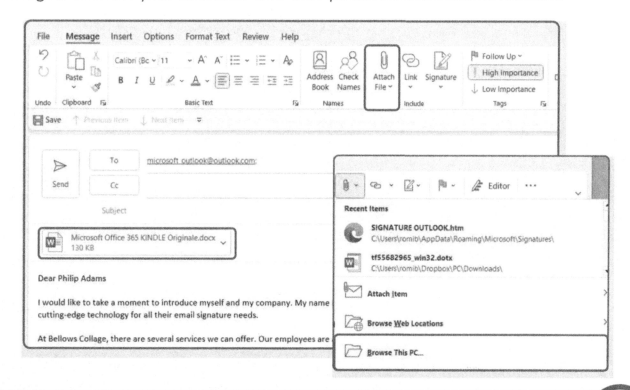

Images in Email Body:

- You can add images directly to the email body
- Not all recipients may see them inline; some may receive them as attachments
- Use ribbon features to add images, similar to other Microsoft applications

Attaching Files:

1. Be aware of attachment size limits (e.g., Gmail allows up to 5GB)
2. Use the "**attach file**" button in the "**home**" or "**insert**" tabs
3. Select from recent files or browse your computer

Alternative Attachment Methods:

- "**Drag and drop**" files into the message window
- "**Copy and paste**" files directly into the message

*"**Pro tip**"*: To remove attachments, simply click on them and press delete on your keyboard.

Important Considerations:

- Image display may vary depending on recipient's email configuration
- Attachment size limits depend on your email service provider
- Multiple attachment methods offer flexibility in file sharing

Automatic Out-of-Office Messages

One of the most valuable features in email is the ability to set up an **automatic reply**, commonly known as an **out of office message**. This function notifies others when you're temporarily unavailable to read or respond to emails, such as during vacations or periods of limited access.

To set up an out of office message, navigate to the **File tab** and select **"Automatic Replies (Out of Office)"** under **Account Information**. In this section, check the box to **"Send automatic replies"**. If you want the message to be sent only during a specific timeframe, select the **"Only send during this time range"** option and set your dates.

Next, compose your message in the provided box. You can include your signature if desired. Remember, even with this feature activated, you'll still have normal access to your incoming messages.

To activate the out of office feature, simply click **"OK"** after writing your message.

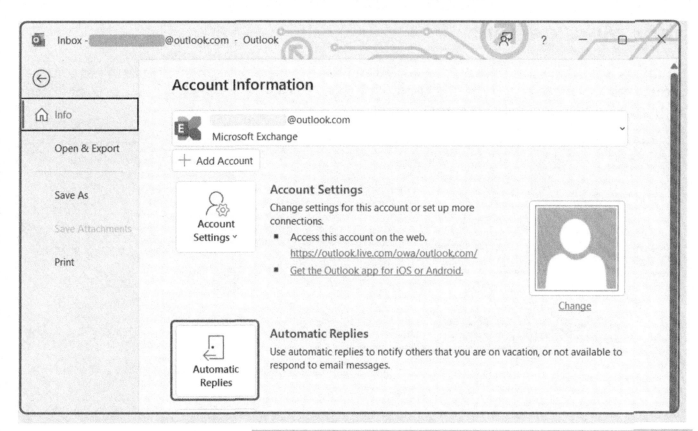

To deactivate your out of office messages, you have two options:

1. Click the **"Turn off"** button on the yellow banner that appears on your Outlook page when you open it.

2. Go to the **File tab** and click **"Turn off"** in the automatic replies section.

This feature ensures that people contacting you are informed about your availability, helping to manage expectations and maintain professional communication even when you're away.

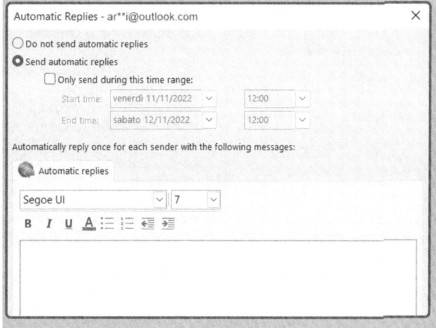

CHAPTER 5

Inbox Management

The **inbox** serves as the primary destination for your incoming messages, unless you've set up **automatic filing**. You have the flexibility to keep all messages in your inbox or organize them into **folders** for easier management.

Home Tab

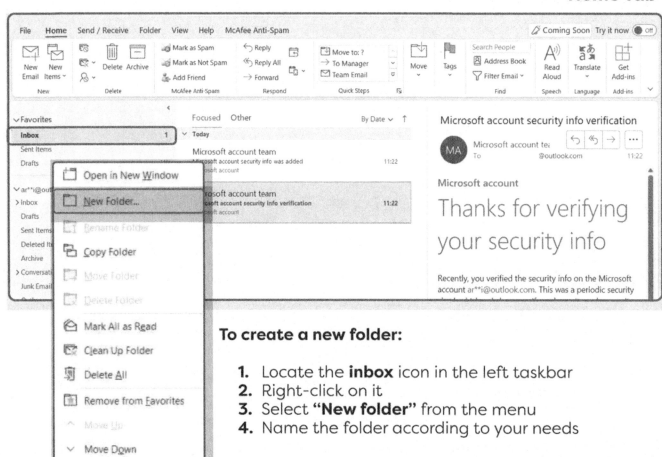

To create a new folder:

1. Locate the **inbox** icon in the left taskbar
2. Right-click on it
3. Select **"New folder"** from the menu
4. Name the folder according to your needs

Once created, you can easily **drag and drop** messages into these folders for better organization.

To **search** for specific messages across your mailbox, use the blue search bar at the top of the window. Enter your keyword, and Outlook will scan both your inbox and folders for relevant messages.

Search Bar

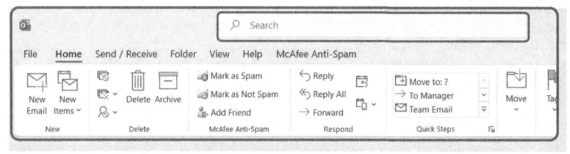

? — □ ✕

Managing Contacts

Creating contacts in Outlook is a straightforward process that can save you time when sending emails. Outlook features a dedicated section for creating **business cards** for your contacts.

To access this feature:

1. Navigate to the bottom of the left taskbar
2. Click on the icon depicting two individuals
3. This opens Outlook's **contacts area**

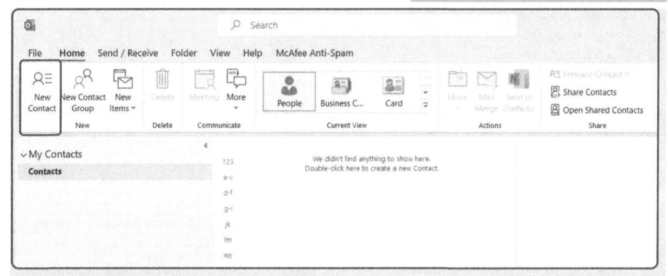

In this section, you can create either a **single contact** or a **group of contacts**. To add a new individual contact:

1. Click the **"New Contact"** button on the far left of the ribbon in the **Home tab**
2. Fill in the relevant information in the new window that appears
3. The contact will then be visible in your contacts section

Contact Information

For additional verification:

1. Start typing the contact's first name in a message
2. Click **"Check Name"**
3. Outlook will search your contacts and fill in the complete information

This feature not only speeds up your email composition but also helps maintain the accuracy of your recipients' information.

Outlook's Calendar

Outlook's **calendar** function is a powerful tool for organizing **appointments** and **meetings**. It provides an easy way to invite others to events or schedule group meetings.

To access the calendar:

1. Click the **calendar icon** at the bottom of the task panel
2. A window displaying a calendar format will appear
3. Use the **"Arrange"** feature in the **Home tab** to customize your calendar view (day, week, or month)

Scheduling Events

To quickly schedule an event:

1. Double-click on the desired date in your calendar
2. In the new window, fill in the event details:

- **Title**: This will be visible in your calendar
- Start and end times (or select "all-day event")
- Check the **"Time zones"** box if working with teams in different time zones

Calendar

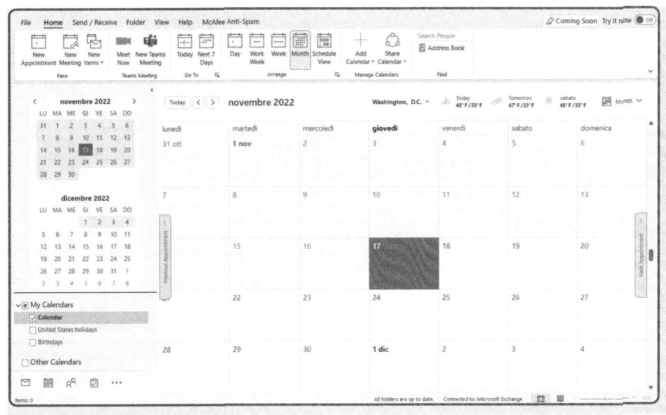

Scheduling Events

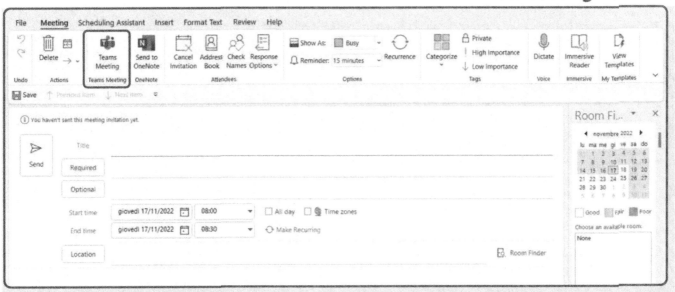

> **Pro tip:** *If you have **Microsoft Teams** installed, you can add a meeting link automatically by clicking the **"Teams Meeting"** icon. All participants will receive the necessary access link.*

For recurring events:

1. Click the **"Recurring"** button
2. Set the repetition schedule

By selecting the **recurring button**, you can specify the days on which the event will repeat itself, as in the case of a **recurring training schedule**. The features that are available on the ribbon can also be used to set up additional features, such as the reminder, the significance of the meeting, and how your day will appear in the calendar.

Creating Tasks

Outlook's **task management** feature, represented by a **flag** icon, allows you to create and track follow-up items.

To flag an email for future action:

1. Go to the **"Tags" section** in the **Home tab** of the ribbon

2. Click the flag button

3. Choose when you want to be reminded about this task

To view your pending tasks:

1. Click the **clipboard with checkmark** icon at the bottom of the inbox pane
2. This opens your to-do list with all pending tasks

To remove a task:

1. Right-click the flagged message
2. Choose to either **"Mark task as complete"** or **"Delete task"**

Pro tip: *Outlook integrates with OneNote, allowing for bi-directional task management:*

- Create tasks in OneNote and send them to Outlook

- Send Outlook items to OneNote:

1. *Select the item you want to transfer*
2. *Click the **"Send to OneNote"** button in the **Home tab***
3. *Choose the destination notebook in the dialog box that appears*

Home Tab

This integration enhances productivity by allowing seamless movement of information be-tween these two powerful organizational tools. The ability to flag emails, set reminders, and sync tasks with OneNote provides a comprehensive system for managing your work and personal responsibilities.

For more details on using OneNote, refer to **Chapter 9** of your guide.

Keyboard Shortcuts on Outlook

Function	PC Shortcut	Mac Shortcut
Close a window	Esc	Command + W
Create new message	Ctrl + Shift + M	Command + N (in mail window)
Send a message	Alt + S	Command + Return
Insert a file	Alt + N, A, F	Command + E
Search for an item	F3	Option + Command + F
Reply to a message	Alt +H, R, P	Command + R
Forward a message	Alt + H, F, W	Command + J
Reply all	Alt + H, R, A	Shift + Command + R
Check for new messages	Ctrl +M or F9	not available
Mail view	Ctrl +1	Command + 1
Calendar view	Ctrl + 2	Command + 2
Contacts view	Ctrl + 3	Command + 3
Tasks view	Ctrl + 4	Command + 4
Notes view	Ctrl + 5	Command + 5
Shortcuts	Ctrl + 7	Command + 7
Next open message	Ctrl + .	Command + ~
Previous open message	Ctrl + ,	Shift + Command + ~
Create appointment	Ctrl + Shift + A	Command + N
Create contact	Ctrl + Shift + C	Command + N
Create note	Ctrl + Shift + N	Command + N

Chapter 6:
Microsoft Skype

Skype, a **communication platform**, stands out among the apps covered in this book as it wasn't originally developed by Microsoft. **Launched in 2003**, Skype was later **acquired by Microsoft in 2011** to replace their Microsoft Live Messenger service.

This versatile software offers users the ability to engage in **video chats**, **instant messaging**, and make **phone calls**. Additionally, Skype supports **file sharing** and **audio transmission**. The app's **multi-platform compatibility** allows users to install it on various devices, including **computers**, **smartphones**, **tablets**, and even **gaming consoles**.

Getting Started:The Basics

The first step to using Skype is **downloading** the app to your device. You can do this by searching for Skype in your device's **app store** or using a web search engine. Once installed, you'll need to **sign in** to your account.

If you already have a **Microsoft account** (like an @outlook.com email), you're all set - no need to create a new one. You can also use your personal email address to set up an account. If you don't have an account yet, use the **create account tool** to make a new one.

Pro Tips:

> 1. To stay connected automatically, check the box that says **"Start Skype as soon as the computer logs on".** This saves you from entering your password each time you use your device.
> 2. Use the **"Remember me"** option to avoid typing your password every time you want to log in.

Configuring Audio and Camera Settings

Before diving into Skype, it's crucial to **verify** your **microphone**, **audio**, and **video settings.** Skype offers a built-in **audio test feature** during your first login. Don't worry if you missed this step initially - you can still access it after connecting.

To **configure** your account settings:

1. Click on your **profile picture** at the top of the **contacts bar**.

2. A **drop-down menu** will appear.

3. Select **Settings** from this menu.

4. In the Settings panel, choose the **Audio and Video** option.

Here, you'll find all the necessary information to **adjust** your audio and video settings. This process ensures your **microphone**, **speakers**, and **camera** are working properly, setting you up for smooth Skype communications.

Customizing Your Skype Profile

While still in the **Settings** menu, you can **personalize** your Skype account with various details. Here's how to make your profile uniquely yours:

1. Navigate to the **Account and Profile** section in the menu.
2. Here, you can add or modify:

- Your display name
- Your profile picture
- Your birthday

This section also allows you to manage other account preferences:

- Toggle the **auto-login** feature for Skype when you sign into your device

- Adjust your **privacy** settings

- Customize the **appearance** of your chat menus

- Set up your preferred **notifications**

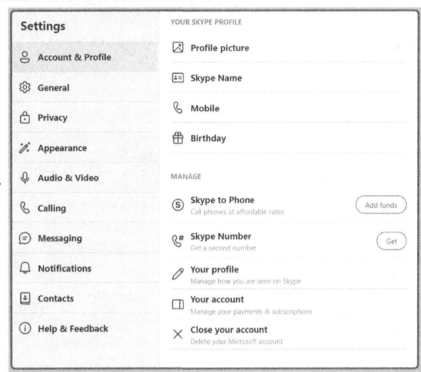

Personalizing these options helps tailor your Skype experience to your needs and preferences. It's worth taking a few minutes to explore these settings, as they can significantly enhance your comfort and efficiency when using the platform.

Remember, you can always return to these settings later if you want to make changes or fine-tune your Skype experience.

Customizing Message Behavior

The **Settings** area of Skype offers even more ways to **personalize** your messaging experience. You can **configure** several default behaviors to suit your preferences and security needs:

- **File Download Settings**: For enhanced **security**, you might want to disable the **automatic download** of received files to your device.

- **Message Formatting**: You can set Skype to automatically format **copied and pasted** text as **quotes** in your chats.

These options, along with many others, can be found and adjusted in the **Messaging** section of Skype's settings.

Adding Contacts: Building Your Skype Network

Skype's true power lies in its ability to connect you with others. To harness this potential, you'll need to build your contact list. Here's a detailed look at how to do that:

1. Searching for Contacts

- Click on the **search button**, typically represented by a magnifying glass icon.
- Enter the name or email address of the person you're looking for.
- Skype will automatically generate a list of potential matches.

2. Understanding Search Results

- Each search result will display:
- The person's name
- Their profile picture (if available)
- Location information
- Number of mutual connections you share
- Under a section labeled **"Group Chats"**, you'll see any previous conversations you've had with this person. As a new user, this section will likely be empty.

3. Inviting New Users to Skype

- If your search doesn't yield results, look for the **"Invite to Skype"** option at the bottom of the results.
- Click this option to send an invitation via email.
- Enter the email address of the person you want to invite.
- Skype will send them a personalized invitation to join the platform.

Managing Your Skype Presence: Status Options

Skype offers a robust status system to help you manage your availability:

1. Status Indicators

- **Active** (Green): You're online and available.

- **Away** (Yellow): You're logged in but may not be at your device.

- **Do Not Disturb** (Red): You're online but don't want to be disturbed.

- **Invisible** (White): You appear offline to others, but can still use Skype.

2. Changing Your Status

- Locate your profile picture or initials in the top-left corner of the Skype window.

- Click on this icon to reveal a dropdown menu.

- Your current status will be the first option below your name.

- Click on your status to see the available options.

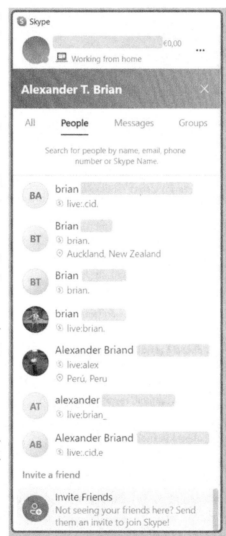
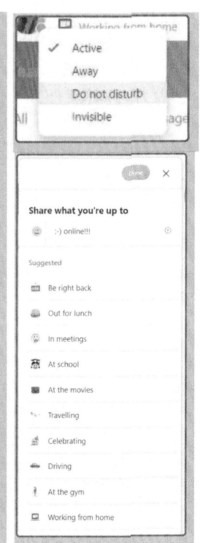

• Select your desired status from the list.

3. **Status Behavior**

- When set to **"Invisible"**, you can see who's online, but others will see you as offline.

- You can still send messages while invisible, which will then show you as online to that specific contact.

- **"Do Not Disturb"** will mute notifications, ideal for when you're in meetings or need to focus.

4. **Automatic Status Changes**

- Skype may automatically change your status to **"Away"** after a period of inactivity.
- You can adjust these settings in the Skype preferences if desired.

Messaging: Initiating Conversations

Skype offers various communication methods, including video calls, audio calls, and text-based chat for both one-on-one and group conversations. Here's how to get started:

1. **Starting a Chat**

- Locate the desired contact in your list.
- Click on their name to open a new conversation window.
- In the **"Type a message"** field at the bottom, begin typing your message.

2. **Advanced Messaging Features** Skype provides several options to enrich your conversations:

- **Contact Sharing**: Send contact information directly through chat.
- **Audio Messages**: Record and send voice messages.
- **Location Sharing**: Share your current location with your contact.
- **Video Messages**: Send short video clips within the chat.
- **Call Scheduling**: Plan future calls with your contacts.
- **Polls**: Create and share polls within your conversations

3. **Switching Communication Modes**

- Look for two blue buttons at the top of the chat window:
- **Camera icon**: Initiates a video call
- **Phone receiver icon**: Starts an audio call

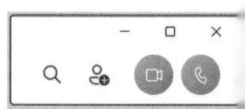

- Clicking these buttons seamlessly transitions you from text chat to video or audio communication.

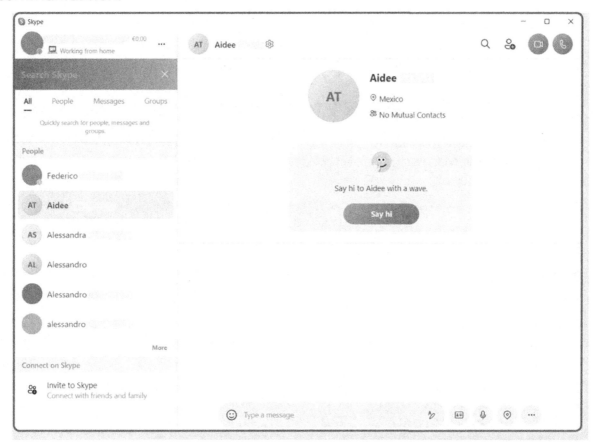

Managing Contacts information

Skype offers several ways to interact with and manage your contacts:

1. **Contact Actions Menu**

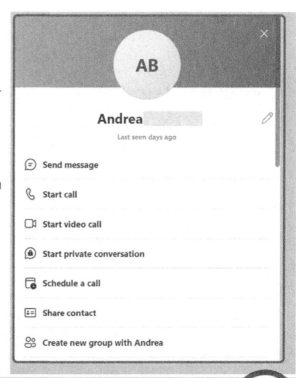

- Click the icon next to a contact's name to open a menu of actions:
- Start a video call
- Initiate an audio call
- Send a file
- Share a contact
- And more...

2. Editing Contact Information

- Look for the **pencil icon** next to the contact's name.

- Clicking this icon allows you to:

  - Customize how the contact's name appears in your list
  - Add or edit their phone number
  - Remove them from your contact list
  - Block the contact

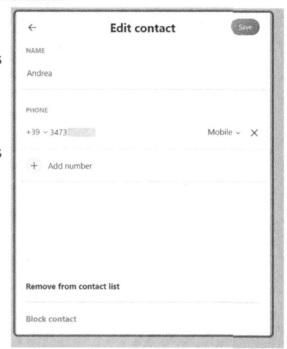

Pro Tip: Managing Blocked Contacts

If you decide to block a contact: They will disappear from your contact list. To un-block them later:

1. *Go to Skype **Settings***
2. *Access the **Contacts** tab*
3. *Select **Blocked Contacts***
4. *Find the contact and choose to unblock them*

This process restores communication with previously blocked contacts.

Creating and Managing Skype Group Chats

Skype offers two straightforward methods for initiating group conversations, enhancing collaboration and social interaction.

1. The first method involves expanding an existing chat. While in a one-on-one conversation, simply click the **"Add Participant"** icon, usually depicted as a person with a plus sign. This allows you to seamlessly include additional contacts in your ongoing discussion. It's particularly useful when you suddenly need input from others during a conversation.

2. The second method starts from scratch. Begin by clicking the **"Chats"** button in the contacts pane, then select **"New Chat"** from the options that appear. A drop-down menu will present various chat types; choose **"New Group Chat"** to proceed. You can

then add participants from your contact list and optionally name the group for easy identification.

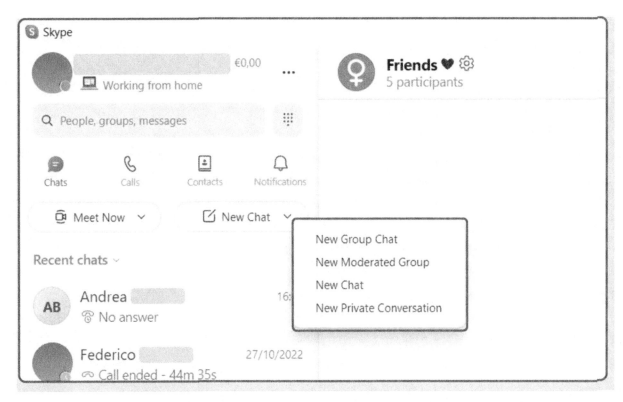

Once created, group chats offer a range of features similar to individual chats. You can share files, initiate video or voice calls, and even create polls. The group creator typically has management privileges, including adding or removing members.

Remember, you can always adjust your notification settings for group chats if they become too active. This flexibility allows you to stay connected without being overwhelmed.

Message Formatting and Emoji Usage in Skype

Text Formatting Options:

1. **Bold**: Makes text stand out for emphasis
2. *Italics*: Useful for subtle emphasis or titles
3. **Strikethrough**: Indicates deleted or corrected text
4. **Link insertion:** Embeds clickable URLs in your message
5. **Code snippets:** Displays text in a monospace font, ideal for sharing code

To access these formatting tools:

- Locate the **letter A with a pen** icon to the right of the message box
- Click this icon to reveal a toolbar with formatting options
- Select your desired format before typing, or highlight existing text to apply formatting

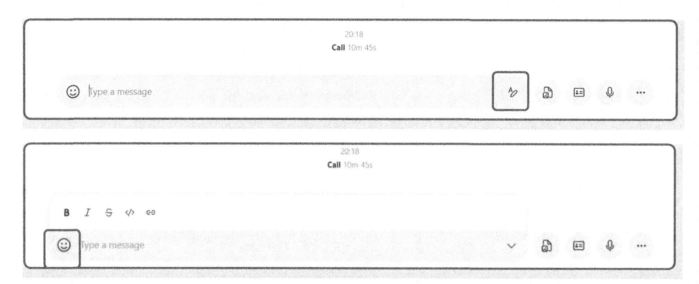

Detailed Formatting Usage:

- Combine formats for more impact (e.g., ***bold and italic***)
- Use code formatting for technical discussions or to preserve text spacing
- When inserting links, Skype often provides a preview, enhancing message context

Emoji Features:

- Click the smiling face icon next to the message box
- Browse through various emoji categories (e.g., smileys, animals, food)
- Skype regularly updates its emoji library to include new and trending emojis
- Use parentheses shortcuts for quick emoji insertion
- Example: **(happy)** automatically converts to a happy face emoji
- **(cat)**, **(pizza)**, **(heart)** are other examples of shortcuts

Emoji Tips:

- Emojis can replace words or punctuation to add emotion to messages
- Be mindful of emoji use in professional contexts
- Emoji meanings can vary across cultures, so use with awareness

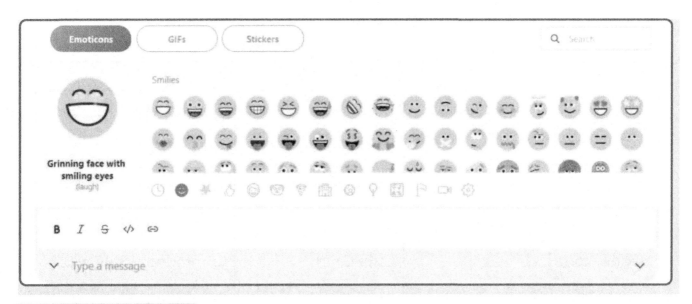

Pro Tip for Line Breaks:

Default setting: **Enter/Return** *key sends the message immediately*
For line breaks without sending:

1. *Press and hold* **Shift**
2. *While holding Shift, press* **Enter** *(PC) or* **Return** *(Mac)*
3. *This creates a new line within the same message*

Use this feature for:

- *Creating lists within a single message*
- *Separating paragraphs in longer messages*
- *Adding space for improved readability*

Additional Messaging Features:

- **File sharing:** Drag and drop files directly into the message box
- **Voice messages:** Record short audio clips when typing isn't convenient
- **Reactions:** Quickly respond to messages with emoji reactions

Keyboard Shortcuts on Skype

Function	PC Shortcut	Mac Shortcut
View keyboard shortcuts	Ctrl + /	Command + /
Open settings	Ctrl + ,	Command + ,
Open themes	Ctrl + T	Command + T
Open or close dark mode	Ctrl + Shift + T	Command + Shift + T
Search contacts	Ctrl + Shift + S	Command + Shift + S
Next conversation	Ctrl + Tab	Command + Tab
Previous conversation	Ctrl + Shift + Tab	Command + Shift + Tab
Zoom in	Ctrl + Shift + +	Command + Shift + +
Zoom out	Ctrl + -	Command + -
Quit Skype	Ctrl + Q	Command + Q
Start new conversation	Ctrl + N	Command + N
Open contacts	Alt + 2	Not available
Add people to conversation	Ctrl + Shift + A	Command + Shift + A
Send a file	Ctrl + Shift + F	Command + Shift + F
Mark as unread	Ctrl + Shift + U	Command + Shift + U
Search within conversation	Ctrl + F	Command + F
Start video call	Ctrl + Shift + K	Command + Shift + K
Mute or unmute conversation	Ctrl + M	Command + M

Chapter 7:
Microsoft Teams

Microsoft Teams was chosen as the **optimal solution** for **enhancing online collaboration** and communication within organizations. While sharing features with Skype, this platform also offers **online file collaboration**, **meeting recording**, and the ability to create **working teams**. Although it includes the Microsoft Suite, a free version is available for download. Microsoft Teams can be used on both **PCs and mobile devices**.

Upon logging in, users are greeted with a **chat window** for communication with team members. Alongside this window are six key buttons: **Activity, Chat, Teams, Calendar, Calls, and Files**. These buttons provide **easy access** to the platform's core functions and enable **seamless integration** with other applications. The following chapter will **examine each of these elements** and explain how to use them effectively.

Create Your First Teams

The first step is understanding how to **create a team** - a group collaborating on a shared topic or organizational unit.

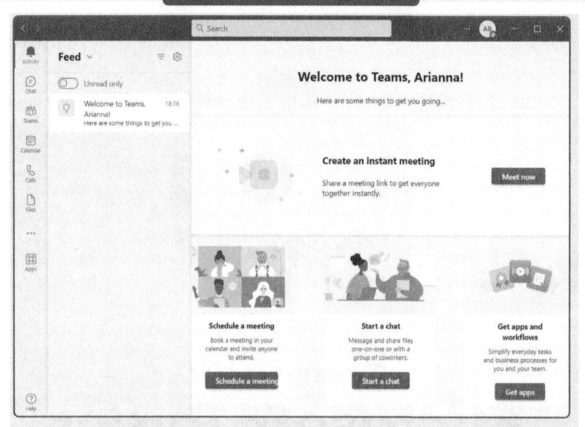

To begin:

1. Click the **Teams** button on the left panel
2. Find the **"Join or create team"** icon at the window's bottom
3. Click the icon

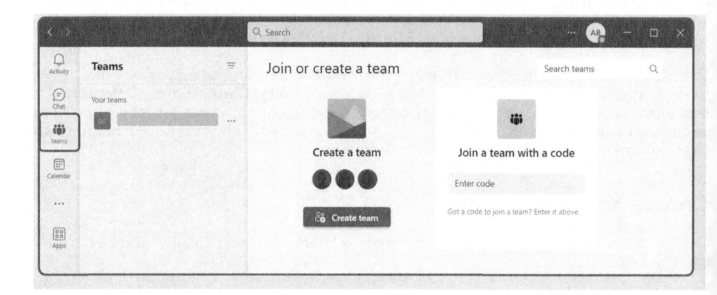

This presents two main options:

- **Create a new team**
- **Join an existing team**

To join with a code, simply enter it in the prompt. To **create a new team**, you have three choices:

1. Start from scratch
2. Base it on an existing group
3. Use a template for scenarios like:

   - Project management
   - Employee onboarding
   - Event planning

Next steps for team creation:

1. Choose between **public** or **private team**
2. **Name your team**
3. Add a **description**
4. Select a **data classification**
5. Start **inviting members**

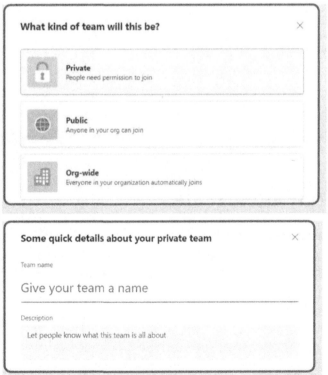

Methods to add people to your team:

- Click the ellipsis next to their name and select **"Add member"**
- For contacts not on your list, enter their email to send an invitation
- **Share a team link** generated through the team's ellipsis button

Pro tip: Teams allows you to designate **team owners** *with special permissions. A team can have multiple owners who can* **add or remove members, add guests,** *and* **modify team settings.** *Other roles include* **members** *and* **guests,** *with permissions set by owners.*

Creating Channels

Channels are essential components of Microsoft Teams, serving as dedicated spaces within a team for topic-specific communication. They help **organize discussions** and enable team members to **collaborate more effectively. Examples of channel usage:**

- **For teachers:**

1. A channel for homework discussions (e.g., "Homework Help")
2. A channel for subject-related questions (e.g., "Physics Q&A")
3. A channel for general student inquiries (e.g., "General Classroom Chat")

- **For businesses:**

1. A channel for project updates (e.g., "Project Alpha Progress")
2. A channel for team announcements (e.g., "Team Announcements")
3. A channel for casual conversation (e.g., "Water Cooler Chat")

Key features of channels:

- Available to all team members unless set as private
- Better organization of topics, reducing clutter in main team conversations
- File uploading and collaboration with version control
- Dedicated chat for each channel, keeping discussions contextual
- Integration with other Microsoft 365 apps like Word, Excel, and PowerPoint

Structure of a channel:

- **Posts tab**: For threaded conversations and announcements
- **Files tab**: For document sharing and real-time collaboration
- **Wiki tab**: For creating and editing shared notes
- Additional tabs can be added for other apps or websites

Creating a new channel:

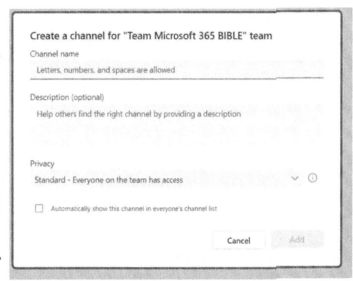

1. Navigate to the team where you want to add a channel

2. Click the ellipsis (**...**) next to the team name

3. Select **"Add channel"**

4. Enter a name and optional description for the channel

5. Choose privacy settings **(Standard or Private)**

6. Click **"Add"** to create the channel

Pro tip: The **Activity** icon on the left panel **highlights** when there's new channel activity. Clicking it shows which groups have updates or movement. Don't worry about locating the source—relevant information is **highlighted** in the window. You can also view **previous notifications**, ensuring you're always up-to-date with your team's communications across all channels.

Uploading/Attach Documents

After creating a channel, you can **share documents** with other users. There are two main methods for **uploading files**:

1. Add them to the chat, which automatically places them in the **Files tab**
2. Go directly to the **Files tab** and upload from there

The Files tab offers additional functionality:

- **Create new documents** for team collaboration
- **Sync** files to ensure all users have the latest versions
- **Download** documents to local devices
- Generate **shareable links** for easy distribution

These features enable **seamless file management** and collaboration within Microsoft Teams channels. The platform's integration of chat and file storage streamlines teamwork and enhances productivity.

If files aren't appearing for all users, the **sync button** can quickly resolve discrepancies, ensuring everyone has access to the most up-to-date information. This robust file-sharing system is a key component of Microsoft Teams' collaborative environment.

Chats and Calls

While Teams is designed for team collaboration, it also excels in **private messaging** and small group chats. This flexibility allows for both team-wide and confidential communications within the same platform.

To add someone to a private conversation:

1. Locate the **person icon** with a plus sign in the top right corner of the chat window
2. Click the icon to open your contact list
3. Search for and select the person you want to add

This feature is particularly useful for bringing in additional team members or experts to an ongoing discussion without creating a new chat thread.

Additional communication features include:

- **Video messaging** (camera icon): Ideal for face-to-face conversations, enhancing personal connection

- **Voice calling** (telephone icon): Perfect for audio-only discussions when visual cues aren't necessary

- **Screen sharing** (square icon with upward arrow): Essential for demonstrations, collaborative document reviews, or visual problem-solving

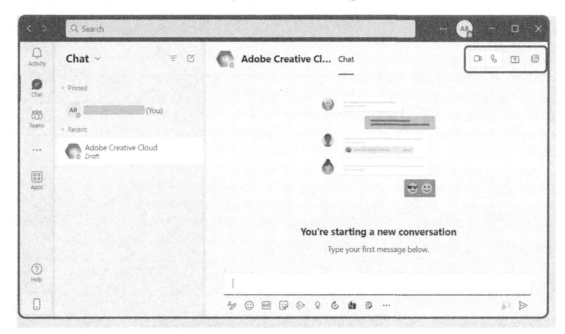

For improved multitasking, you can **pop out** chat windows. This feature allows you to:

- View multiple conversations simultaneously
- Keep important chats visible while working in other applications
- Easily reference information from one chat while participating in another

Sending Messages and Files

Teams offers **advanced text formatting** options, surpassing many other messaging platforms. When composing a message, you can:

- Use **bold**, *italic*, and underline for emphasis
- Change font color and style to highlight important information
- Use bullet points and numbering for organized lists or step-by-step instructions

These formatting options help convey tone and importance in written communication, crucial for clear messaging in a digital workspace.

To set message importance, use the **exclamation mark icon.** This feature is useful for urgent communications or critical announcements.

The trash can icon in the formatting toolbox allows quick deletion of draft messages, saving time when you need to start over.

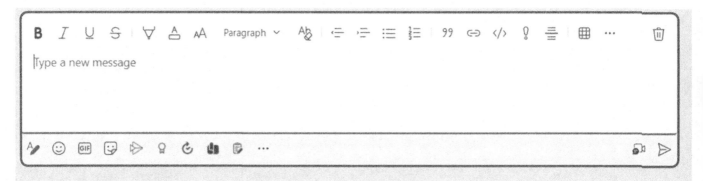

Message Features

- The '@' **symbol** is a powerful tool for:

  - Mentioning specific users to get their attention
  - Ensuring important messages aren't overlooked in busy channels
  - Directing questions or tasks to the right team member

- The **Reply** function creates threaded conversations, which:

  - Keeps related messages grouped together
  - Makes it easier to follow specific topics within a busy channel
  - Reduces clutter in the main channel feed

- **File sharing** via drag and drop:

1. Simply drag a file from your computer into the message area
2. The file appears in the conversation for immediate access
3. It's automatically added to the channel's **Files** section for easy future reference

This dual-storage approach ensures that important documents are both immediately accessible and properly organized for long-term use.

> **Pro tip:** *To notify everyone in a channel, use '@' followed by the channel name. This feature:*

- Alerts all users without the need to select them individually
- Is ideal for important announcements or time-sensitive information
- Should be used judiciously to avoid notification fatigue

By leveraging these features, teams can communicate more effectively, ensuring that the right information reaches the right people at the right time, all within the Microsoft Teams environment

Meeting Features

Microsoft Teams' meetings feature is one of its most comprehensive and sophisticated components. This section will reveal the wide array of options available when hosting a meeting through the platform.

You'll discover how to use Teams to its fullest potential for online meetings, including:

- Inviting attendees
- Adding participants
- Sharing your screen
- Customizing your background
- Recording sessions

And that's just the beginning. Keep reading to explore all the capabilities that Microsoft Teams offers for your virtual meetings. **You'll be amazed at how Teams can enhance your online collaboration experience.**

Scheduling and Starting a Meeting

Teams and Outlook work together seamlessly, allowing you to sync information and keep your **calendar** current with all your upcoming meetings. While scheduling a Teams meeting automatically updates your Outlook calendar, you're not limited to using the email service for booking meetings.

To schedule a meeting directly in Teams:

1. **Locate the calendar icon** on the left sidebar of the Teams window.
2. Click on it to view your availability.
3. To create a new meeting, **click the "+ new meeting" button** at the top of the window.
4. **Fill in the meeting details**, including:

- Meeting name
- Participants
- Date and time
- Specific channel (if applicable)
- Optional personalized message

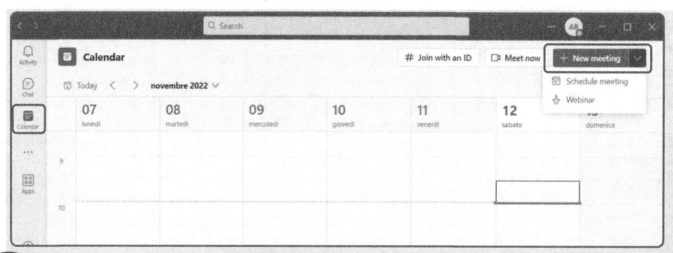

The process closely resembles scheduling in Outlook, so we won't delve into every detail. The key information you'll need to provide includes the meeting's name, participants, date and time, and any specific channel it will be held in. While you have the option to add a personalized message to the invite, it's not required.

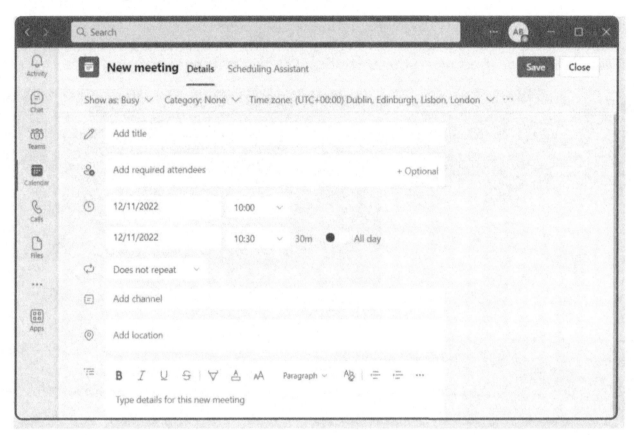

Pro tip: *On the meeting invite's top menu, you can manage the meeting's time zone information and **response options.** This feature is especially helpful if you are working with people who are located in different regions because it allows you to specify how the invitees can respond and the time for the meeting.*

Joining and Customizing Your Meeting Experience

As your scheduled meeting approaches, Teams will notify you it's about to begin. If you're the organizer, you'll need to admit participants waiting in the lobby. When you click join, you'll have the opportunity to set your initial audio and video preferences.

Don't worry if you need to change these settings later - you can adjust them at any time during the meeting.

Customizing Your Background

If your surroundings aren't ideal for a professional meeting, Teams offers background options:

1. Click the **background filters** button below your video preview.
2. Choose to blur your background or select from Teams' standard templates.
3. Once you're satisfied with your settings, click the **join now** button on the far right to

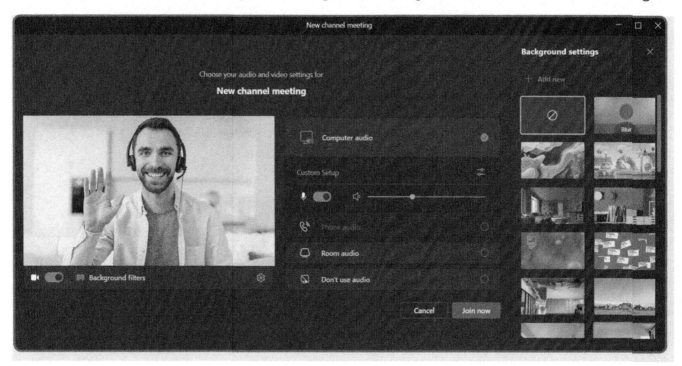

enter the meeting.

> **Pro tip:** For a more personalized touch in corporate settings, you can add custom backgrounds like your company logo. Just click **add new** at the top of the background list to create your own template.

Setting Up Meeting Parameters

When organizing a Teams meeting, **you have a range of options to customize the experience** and control participant interactions. You can:

- Set the meeting duration
- Assign participant roles
- Control screen sharing and file sharing permissions
- Removing participants

- Admitting users from the lobby
- Starting or stopping recording

Manage these options through the **meeting options** button in the calendar. **Defining roles such as organizer, co-organizer, presenter, and attendee determines each participant's capabilities** during the meeting.

To manage these options:

1. Go to your Teams **calendar**
2. Select the meeting you want to configure
3. Click the **meeting options** button
4. Adjust settings as needed for your specific meeting requirements

*Pro tip: For recurring meetings, you can **save these settings as a template**. This allows you to quickly apply the same configuration to future meetings, saving time and ensuring consistency.*

During the Meeting

During a Teams meeting, participants have access to various **interactive tools**. Let's explore these features in depth:

Top Bar Navigation: The top of your meeting window houses several crucial icons:

- **Participants list**: View all attendees, useful for large meetings or tracking attendance.

- **Chat window**: Opens a side panel for text communication, perfect for sharing links or asking questions without interrupting the speaker.

- **Raise hand** feature: Signals to the host that you have a question or comment, maintaining meeting order.

- **Pop out** option: Allows you to separate the meeting window, helpful for multi-tasking or dual-monitor setups.

The Powerful Ellipsis (...) Menu: This menu, especially vital for organizers, offers advanced features:

- **Recording**: Captures video and audio of the entire meeting.

  - *Pro tip: Inform participants when you start recording for privacy reasons.*

  - Recordings are saved in the chat files and can be shared via Teams or OneDrive.

- **Real-time captions**: Transcribes spoken words into text on-screen.

  - Enhances accessibility for hearing-impaired participants or in noisy environments.

  - Useful for non-native speakers to follow along more easily.

- **Live translation**: Translates captions into different languages in real-time.

  - Breaks down language barriers in international meetings.

  - Currently supports a limited number of languages, but the list is expanding.

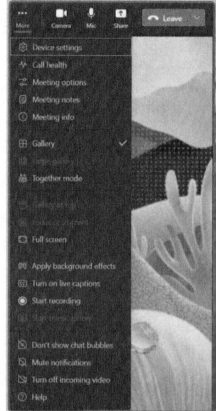

Dynamic Meeting Management:

- **Role changes**: Access **"meeting options"** to adjust participant roles on the fly.

  - Useful for promoting a participant to presenter for their portion of the meeting.

- **Meeting notes**: Collaborative note-taking feature accessible during and after the meeting.

  - Great for recording action items, decisions, or key points.
  - Notes are automatically saved and shared with all participants.

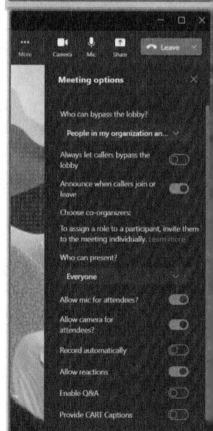

? — ☐ ✕

Content Sharing Capabilities:

The **share button** unlocks various presentation options:

- **Window sharing**: Share a specific application window.

  - Ensures privacy by not displaying your entire screen.

- **PowerPoint sharing**: Present slides with enhanced features.

  - Attendees can navigate slides independently, great for self-paced review.
  - Presenter can still control the main presentation view.

- **Whiteboard**: Opens a digital canvas for real-time collaboration.

  - Ideal for brainstorming sessions or visual explanations.
  - All participants can contribute simultaneously.

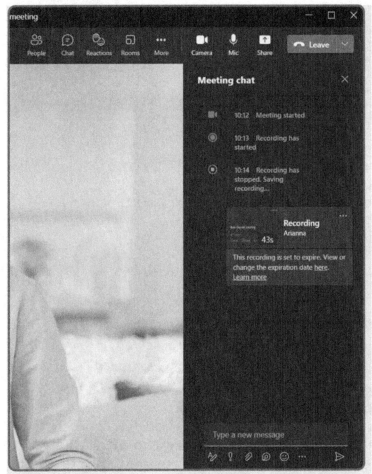

Recording a Meeting

Share content

Pro tip: *When sharing a PowerPoint directly through Teams, you benefit from smoother transitions and lower bandwidth usage compared to sharing your screen while running PowerPoint.*

Wrapping Up Your Teams Meeting

As your meeting comes to a close, Teams offers several important features to ensure a smooth conclusion:

Attendance Tracking:

- Before exiting, you can download an **attendee list**.
- This feature provides a **record of participants** who joined the meeting.
- **Important:** This must be done **before the session ends**, as the list isn't accessible afterward.

Meeting Conclusion Options:

Teams distinguishes between two ways to exit a meeting:

1. **Ending the Meeting:**

   - This action closes the session for all participants.
   - Typically used by the organizer when the meeting is completely over.
   - Ends all ongoing conversations and screen shares.
   - Use this option for a definitive conclusion to prevent lingering participants.

2. **Leaving the Meeting:**

   - This allows you to exit while others continue.
   - Ideal when you need to step out but the discussion isn't over.
   - The meeting remains active for other participants.

- **Useful for:**

  - Facilitators who set up the meeting but don't need to stay
  - Participants who have conflicting appointments

By understanding these options, you can **manage your meetings more effectively**, ensuring proper closure or continuity as needed. Remember, your choice between ending and leaving can significantly impact the meeting's flow and participants' expectations.

MICROSOFT TEAMS

Post-Meeting Resources:

- **Recordings** are automatically processed and stored in the chat files.

  - Easily accessible for review or for those who missed the live meeting.

- **Sharing options:**

  - **Internal:** Share link directly through Teams.

  - **External:** Download and upload to One-Drive for secure external sharing.

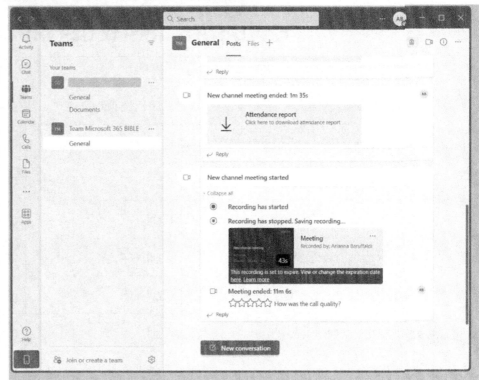

Keyboard Shortcuts on Teams

Function	PC Shortcut	Mac Shortcut
Search or access command bar	Ctrl + E	Command + E
Start a new chat	Ctrl + N	Command + N
Open settings	Ctrl + ,	Command + ,
Toggle mute	Ctrl + Shift + M	Command + Shift + M
Toggle video	Ctrl + Shift + O	Command + Shift + O
Start a call	Ctrl + Shift + K	Command + Shift + K
Show keyboard shortcuts	Ctrl + Shift + H	Command + Shift + H
Show commands	Ctrl + .	Command + .

Keyboard Shortcuts on Teams

Function	PC Shortcut	Mac Shortcut
Navigate to Activity	Ctrl + 1	Command + 1
Navigate to Chat	Ctrl + 2	Command + 2
Navigate to Teams	Ctrl + 3	Command + 3
Navigate to Calendar	Ctrl + 4	Command + 4
Navigate to Calls	Ctrl + 5	Command + 5
Navigate to Files	Ctrl + 6	Command + 6
Go to	Ctrl + G	Command + G
Raise or lower hand	Ctrl + Shift + E	Command + Shift + E
Decline call	Ctrl + Shift + D	Command + Shift + D
Accept call	Ctrl + Shift + A	Command + Shift + A
Take a screenshot	Ctrl + Shift + S	Command + Shift + S
Toggle share tray	Ctrl + Shift + Space	Command + Shift + Space
Toggle fullscreen	Ctrl + Shift + F	Command + Shift + F
Expand compose box	Ctrl + Shift + X	Command + Shift + X
Start a new line	Shift + Enter	Shift + Return
Mention someone	@	@
Increase font size	Ctrl + Shift + >	Command + Shift + >
Decrease font size	Ctrl + Shift + <	Command + Shift + <

Chapter 8:
Microsoft OneDrive

Your Cloud Storage Solution

OneDrive, Microsoft's **cloud storage** solution, offers a **comprehensive platform** for storing various types of **digital content**. Users can save documents, photos, and music files while enjoying **easy access** from any cloud-connected device. As part of the **Microsoft Suite**, users receive a generous **1 terabyte** of initial storage space.

A **standout feature** of OneDrive is its ability to **sync with your computer's settings**, enabling **automatic cloud backup** of new files without manual saving to your local drive. While similar to services like **Google Drive**, OneDrive sets itself apart through its **enhanced functionality** and **seamless integration** with Microsoft Office applications.

The **cloud-based approach** of OneDrive brings several **advantages**, including **cross-device access** to files, ample storage, and **auto-save options**. These features, combined with its **deep integration** into the **Microsoft ecosystem**, make OneDrive a **powerful tool** for **boosting productivity** and ensuring **constant file availability**. In the following sections, we'll dive into the main **benefits** and **best practices** for maximizing your use of OneDrive, helping you get the most out of your **cloud storage experience**.

Accessing OneDrive-In

To use OneDrive, simply **search** for it in your web browser and click the appropriate link. **Logging in** requires the email address you used to sign up and your password. This should be the same credentials you use for other Microsoft programs, allowing the system to **identify your account** and sync your documents.

If you've logged in previously, your password may be saved, requiring only a click to continue. For **enhanced security**, consider activating **two-factor authentication**. This sends a unique code to your phone each time you log in. While optional, it's **highly recommended** to protect your important files from unauthorized access.

> **Pro tip:** Don't worry if you didn't set up your initial information perfectly. You can always **access your account settings** to modify any details, including **security information** and other account preferences.

File Management in OneDrive

When you first launch OneDrive, you'll be greeted by a **comprehensive dashboard** that serves as your central hub for file management. This interface is designed to provide quick access to your most important content and features:

1. **Main Content Area:**

   - Displays your primary folders and recent files
   - Provides a visual overview of your cloud storage organization
   - Allows for quick identification of frequently accessed items

2. Left Sidebar Navigation:

- **Files**: Access all your stored documents and folders
- **Recent**: Quickly view and open recently modified or uploaded files
- **Photos**: A dedicated section for your image files, often with preview capabilities
- **Shared**: Easy access to files others have shared with you or that you've shared
- **Recycle Bin**: Retrieve accidentally deleted files or permanently remove them

3. Top Blue Bar:

- Offers seamless integration with other Microsoft online applications
- Enables quick switching between OneDrive and programs like Word, Excel, or PowerPoint

4. Toolbar:

- Located just below the blue bar
- Provides quick access to essential OneDrive functions like upload, sync, and share

Creating and Editing Files in the Cloud

The **"+ New"** button is your gateway to content creation within OneDrive:

1. Document Creation Options:

- **Word**: For text documents, reports, and letters
- **Excel**: Spreadsheets for data analysis and calculations
- **PowerPoint**: Presentation slides for meetings and pitches

- **OneNote**: Digital notebooks for note-taking and organization
- **Forms**: For creating surveys and questionnaires
- **Plain Text**: Simple, unformatted text documents
- **Folders**: To organize your files into logical groups

2. Online Editing:

- Clicking on any of these options opens the online version of the software

- These web apps closely mimic their desktop counterparts, with most essential features available

- Changes are automatically saved to the cloud, ensuring your work is always up-to-date and accessible

3. File Location:

- New files can be created directly in the main workspace or within specific folders
- This flexibility allows for immediate organization of your documents

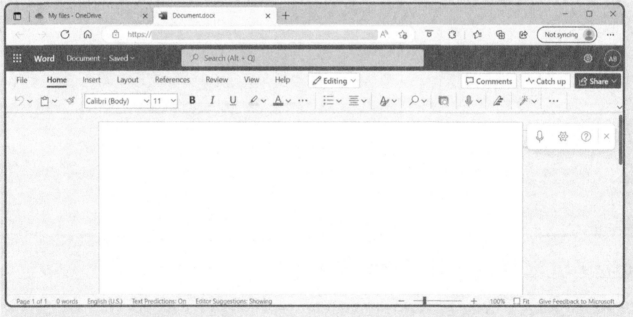

Online Word Document

Advanced File Operations

Right-clicking on any file or folder name reveals a wealth of options:

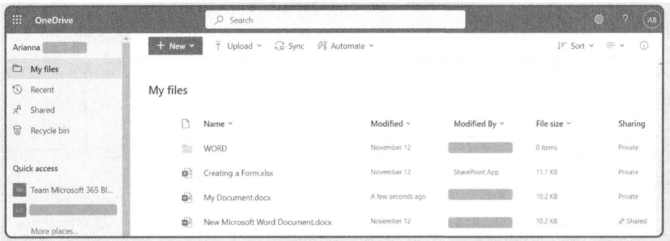

MICROSOFT ONEDRIVE

1. File Management:

- **Preview/Open**: Quickly view contents without fully opening the file
- **Download**: Save a local copy to your device
- **Delete**: Move items to the Recycle Bin
- **Move/Copy**: Reorganize your files within OneDrive
- **Rename**: Change file names directly in the cloud

2. Collaboration Tools:

- **Share**: Grant access to others, with customizable permissions
- **Version History**: View and restore previous versions of your documents

3. File Information:

- **Details**: View comprehensive metadata about your files
- **Modification History**: Track changes and edits over time

Uploading and Downloading Documents

To **add content** to your OneDrive, you'll find a convenient upload option located right beside the **"+ New" button** on the main dashboard.

This feature offers flexibility in your upload choices, allowing you to select either individual files or entire folders for storage.

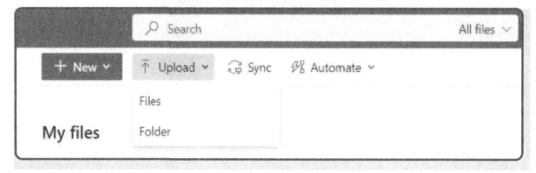

Here are the primary methods for uploading:

- **Using the Upload Button:** Located next to the "+ New" button on the home page. Offers two options: **Upload a file** - **Upload a folder**

  1. Click the upload button
  2. Choose file or folder option
  3. Navigate your computer's file system
  4. Select the item(s) to upload
  5. Confirm the upload

- **Drag and Drop Method:** A faster, more intuitive approach

  1. Open OneDrive in one window
  2. Open the folder containing your file in another window
  3. Click and hold the file you want to upload
  4. Drag it into the OneDrive window
  5. Release to drop the file in the desired location

- A status bar will appear, showing upload progress

Pro Tip: *The drag and drop functionality is universal within OneDrive. Use it to: Upload new files, Move files between folders, Reorganize your cloud storage structure.*

Downloading Documents from OneDrive

To retrieve files from OneDrive to your local device:

1. **Select the File:**

   - Click the circle next to the file name to select it
   - The top toolbar will update with new options once a file is selected

? — □ ✕

2. Initiate Download:

- Click the "Download" button in the updated toolbar
- Alternatively, right-click the file and choose "Download" from the context menu

3. Choose Download Location:

- A dialog box will open
- Navigate to your preferred save location on your computer
- Select the folder and confirm

4. Monitor Download:

- Most browsers show download progress in their interface
- Once complete, you can access the file locally

<u>Other Options</u>

Advanced Sharing Features

When you select a file in OneDrive, the top toolbar expands to reveal additional functionalities. A key feature here is the **"Share" button**. Clicking this opens a dialog box where you can:

- Enter email addresses of intended recipients
- Compose a personalized message
- Generate a shareable link

Once shared, the file's status changes from "private" to "shared", indicating multiple users now have access.

You have control over the **level of access** granted to others. When sharing, you can set permissions by clicking the pen icon next to the recipient's email. Choose between "can edit"

and "can view" to define their interaction with the document. These permissions can be adjusted later if needed.

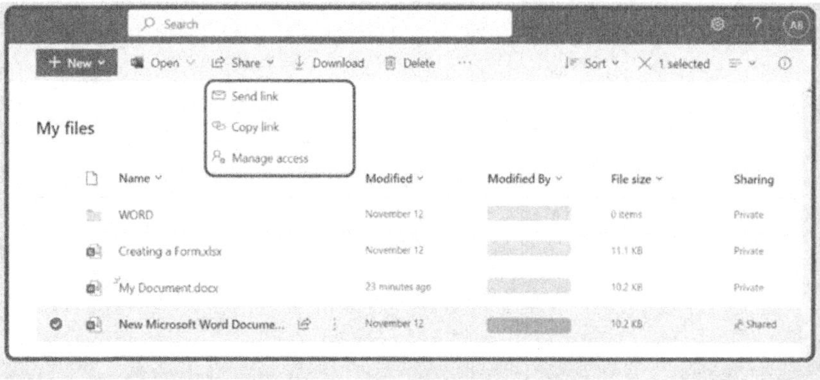

Pro Tip: *OneDrive allows multi-selection of files and folders. The available actions in the toolbar will vary depending on your selection combination (file-file, file-folder, or folder-folder).*

Embedding Files

For those with personal or business websites, OneDrive offers an **embedding feature**. After selecting a file or folder, click the **"</> Embed"** button. This generates an HTML code in a side panel, which you can add to your webpage to display OneDrive content directly.

Important Note: Embedded files or folders are publicly viewable without requiring sign-in. Exercise caution and only embed content that's safe for public access.

This embedding capability enhances OneDrive's versatility, allowing for seamless integration of your cloud-stored content with your online presence. However, it's crucial to consider privacy implications when using this feature, especially for sensitive or confidential information.

Synchronization

OneDrive's integration with the Microsoft Suite brings powerful **automatic synchronization** capabilities to your digital workflow. If you have the Microsoft Suite installed on your computer, OneDrive typically comes pre-configured, ready to sync your files effortlessly.

When set up correctly, this **seamless integration** means that any new document you create, file you save, or modification you make on your local device is automatically mirrored in your OneDrive cloud storage. This two-way synchronization extends to online edits as well.

If you make changes to a document through OneDrive's web interface, these updates will be reflected when you next open the file on your local device.

This **bi-directional sync** feature offers remarkable flexibility in how and where you work. It enables you to:

- Access your latest files from any device with internet connectivity
- Work on documents remotely, even without your primary computer
- Collaborate in real-time with colleagues, with changes visible to all parties

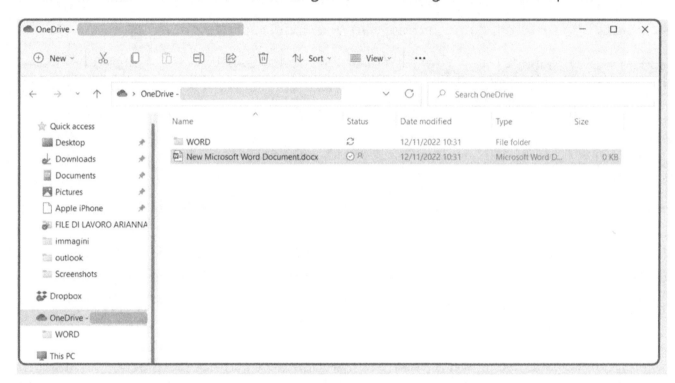

Pro Tip: OneDrive uses a subtle but effective visual cue to alert you to recent changes. When a document has been newly added or modified in OneDrive, you'll notice **three blue dashes** appear next to its name in the file list. This quick indicator helps you easily identify which files have been recently updated or added to your cloud storage.

Cloud-Based Backup Solution

OneDrive serves a dual purpose as both a cloud storage platform and an automatic back-up solution. In essence, the files you store in OneDrive are already backed up, eliminating the need for additional backup procedures. This feature proves particularly useful even if you don't regularly access your files in the cloud.

CHAPTER 8

One of OneDrive's standout features is its **persistent file retention**. Even if you permanently delete a file from your local device using the **Shift + Delete** command, a copy remains accessible in OneDrive's cloud-based **recycle bin**. This safeguard provides a safety net against accidental deletions.

To recover mistakenly deleted files:

1. Visit the OneDrive website
2. Locate and click the **"Recycle Bin"** option in the left sidebar
3. Find the deleted file in question
4. Select and restore it to both the cloud and your local device

Storage Capacity Management

OneDrive typically provides new users with a generous **1 TB** of initial storage. You can easily monitor your storage usage via a **progress bar** located at the bottom of the left task pane. This blue line visually represents your used space relative to your total available storage. The information is presented both graphically and numerically, offering a clear overview of your storage situation.

> *Pro Tip: For users who require additional space, OneDrive offers options to **expand storage capacity**. To purchase more storage:*

1. Access the **"Options"** menu
2. Select your desired additional storage amount
3. The cost will be automatically billed monthly to the credit card associated with your account

For a more detailed analysis of your storage usage, navigate to the **"Manage Storage"** section within the Options menu. This provides comprehensive insights into how your cloud space is being utilized.

Account Settings

To **modify or view** your OneDrive **account settings**, follow these steps:

1. Look for your **initials in a circle** in the **top right corner** of the program window.

2. Click this icon.

3. Choose **"View Account"**.

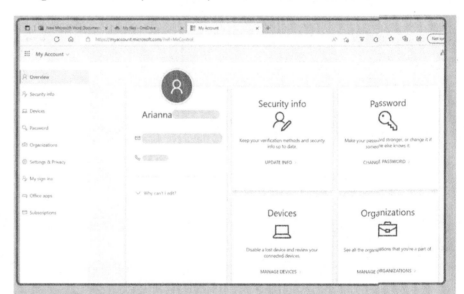

In this account section, you can manage several aspects of your Microsoft account:

1. **Security and Privacy:**

   - Change your password
   - Manage privacy settings
   - Adjust security options, including:
   - Enabling two-factor authentication
   - Setting up security questions
   - Managing trusted devices

2. **Device and Product Management:**

   - View devices with Microsoft Suite installed
   - Review your **purchased Microsoft products**
   - **Update payment methods** for future purchases

3. **Additional Features:**

   - **Add family members** to your Microsoft plan
   - Use **Outlook online** without needing your original device
   - **Explore other Microsoft services**, such as: Xbox Live, Microsoft 365 apps, Skype

Microsoft Forms - Bonus Section:

When exploring OneDrive to initiate a new file, you may have noticed a program that hasn't been mentioned before: **Microsoft Forms**. This tool is worth explaining, as it's a valuable part of the Microsoft suite.

Microsoft Forms serves as the company's solution for creating **online surveys and quizzes**. This versatile application allows users to craft personalized questionnaires and distribute them to others, making it ideal for conducting studies or gathering feedback. One of its key advantages is that all results are automatically stored in your OneDrive, ensuring easy access whenever you need to review the data.

A standout feature of Microsoft Forms is its **real-time functionality**. As participants respond to your questions, the results update instantly, providing you with up-to-the-minute insights. However, if you prefer to control the duration of your survey or quiz, the platform also offers the flexibility to set specific start and end dates.

This seamless integration with OneDrive makes Microsoft Forms a powerful tool for creating, sharing, and analyzing various types of questionnaires.

Creating a Form

1. **Access Microsoft Forms:**

   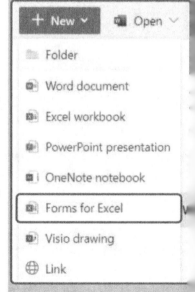

   - Open OneDrive and click the **+ New** button
   - Select **Forms** from the dropdown menu
   - A new window will open, taking you to the Forms start page

2. **Set Up Your Form:**

   - Add a **form title**: This is the main heading for your form
   - (Optional) Add a **form description**: Use this to explain the purpose of your survey or provide instructions
   - Edit these by clicking on

Adding Questions

1. Click the **Add new** button to choose a question type:

   - **Choice**: Multiple choice or checkbox questions
   - **Text**: Short or long answer text fields
   - **Rating**: Star rating or numeric scale
   - **Date**: Calendar-based date selection

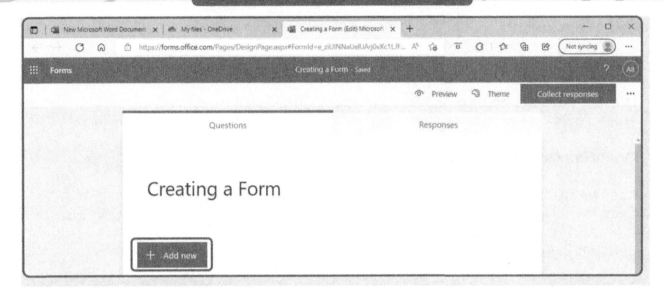

2. Customizing Choice Questions:

- Enter your question in the **Question** field
- Add answer options in the fields below
- Click **+ Add option** to include more choices
- Select **Add "Other" option** to allow custom responses

3. Question Settings:

- **Multiple answers**: Allow respondents to select more than one option
- **Required**: Make the question mandatory
- **Subtitle**: Add extra context or instructions for the question

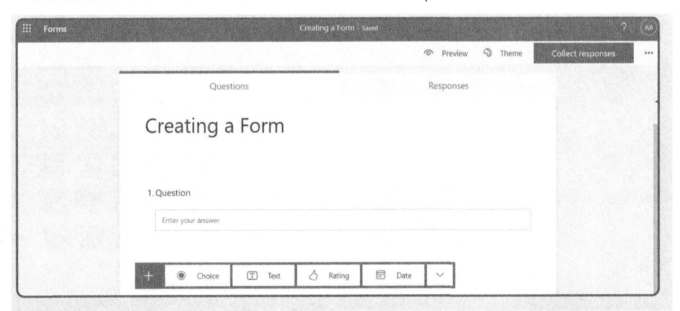

Advanced Features

1. Branching Logic:

- Use the **Add branching** option to create conditional questions
- This allows you to show different questions based on previous answers

2. Question Reordering:

- Use the up/down arrows or drag-and-drop to reorder questions
- Click the ellipsis (...) button for more options like duplicating or deleting questions

3. Section Breaks:

- Add sections to group related questions together
- This can make longer forms more manageable

Finalizing Your Form

1. Preview:

- Click the **Preview** button to see how your form looks to respondents
- Test your form to ensure all questions and logic work as expected

2. Theming:

- Select **Theme** to customize the look of your form
- Choose from pre-set color schemes or add your own background image

3. Sharing:

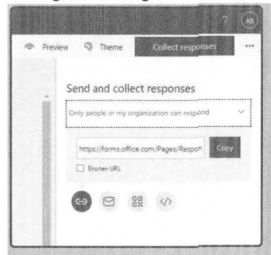

- Click **Send** to get sharing options
- You can share via:
- Direct link
- QR code
- Embed code for websites
- Email

4. Response Handling:

- View responses in the **Responses** tab
- See summary data in graph format
- Download responses to Excel for detailed analysis

Pro Tips:

1. Use **Question Branching** to create personalized paths through your form
2. Leverage **Microsoft Forms AI** for suggested questions based on your form title
3. Regularly check the **Responses** tab for real-time updates as people complete your form
4. Utilize the **Share to collaborate** feature to work on forms with colleagues
5. Consider using **Forms Pro** for advanced features like workflow automation and deeper analytics

Remember, Microsoft Forms automatically saves your work, so you can come back and edit your form at any time. Happy form creating!

Keyboard Shortcuts on One Drive

Function	PC Shortcut	Mac Shortcut
Select all items	Ctrl + A	Command + A
Copy selected items	Ctrl + C	Command + C
Cut selected items	Ctrl + X	Command + X
Paste items	Ctrl + V	Command + V
Delete selected item	Delete	Delete
Rename selected item	F2	Enter
Refresh the page	F5	Command + R
Create a new folder	Ctrl + Shift + N	Command + Shift + N
Open selected item	Enter	Command + O
Select multiple items	Ctrl + Click	Command + Click
Select a range of items	Shift + Click	Shift + Click
Move up one level	Backspace	Command + Up Arrow
Search	Ctrl + E	Command + E
Toggle item preview pane	Alt + P	Option + P
Toggle details pane	Alt + Shift + P	Option + Shift + P
Open context menu	Shift + F10	Control + Click
Close OneDrive	Alt + F4	Command + Q
Open OneDrive settings	Ctrl + ,	Command + ,
Undo last action	Ctrl + Z	Command + Z
Redo last action	Ctrl + Y	Command + Shift + Z
Move selected items	Ctrl + Shift + V	Command + Option + V

Chapter 9:
Microsoft OneNote

OneNote is a **digital notebook** feature within the Microsoft Suite that allows you to **take notes** and **integrate information** with Microsoft Outlook. This software enables you to **organize** various types of information in **notebooks**, ranging from recipes to work or school-related content. A unique feature of OneNote is its **drawing capability**, which transforms your device into a virtual sketchpad for any designs you wish to create.

Let's begin with the basics: **creating a notebook** and **customizing its organization** to suit your needs.

Creating a Notebook

When you launch OneNote, you'll be prompted to create a new notebook or open an existing one. Let's say you want to start fresh - your first step is to **name your notebook**. Once named, the program opens to a blank page with the ribbon hidden. To make navigation easier, click on the **home tab** of the ribbon, expand it, and pin it to the top. As a quick reminder from chapter one: after expanding the ribbon, pin it by clicking the thumbnail on the far right of the task pane.

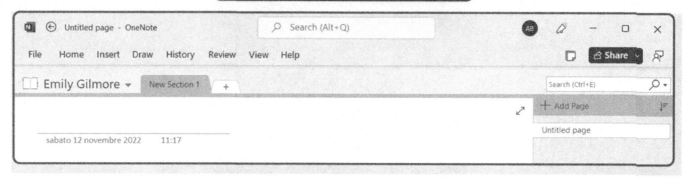

Home Tab

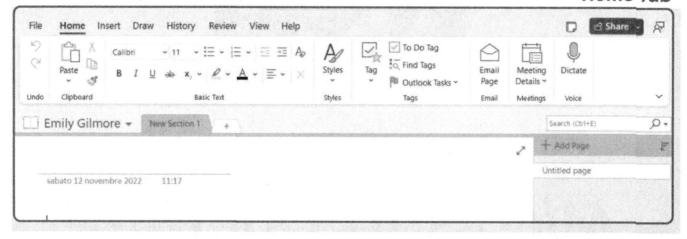

You'll notice the ribbon looks similar to other Microsoft Suite programs, making it **user-friendly**. OneNote offers familiar tools like **font formatting**, **copy and paste** functions, and **bullet or numbered lists**. The review pane is also available, providing **translation** and **spellcheck** features.

When you first open your notebook, you'll see a colored tab representing a **section**. To rename this section, double-click its name and type a relevant label. For instance, if you're creating a kitchen notebook, you might label it **"recipes"**.

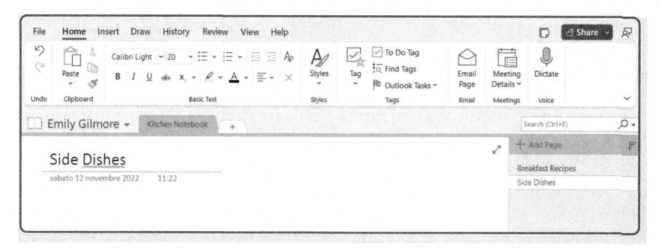

The first line on the page is for your **page title**. Continuing our example, you could enter a dish name here. To add more pages to this section - and you can add as many as you want - click the **"add page"** button at the top of the pane on the **right** side of your screen.

> **Pro tip**: Don't worry about renaming pages - OneNote will do this **automatically** based on what you type in the title line of each page.

Creating and Editing Sections and Pages

Let's say you want to expand your notebook beyond recipes, but you want to keep things organized. You can do this by creating additional **sections**. Here's how:

1. **Create a new section:**

- Look for the **+** button next to the first color-coded tab.
- Click on it to automatically create a new section with a default color.

2. **Customize section color (optional):**

- Right-click on the new tab.
- Choose your preferred color from the options presented.

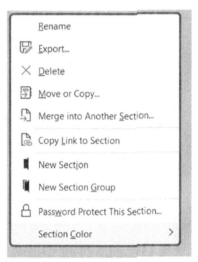

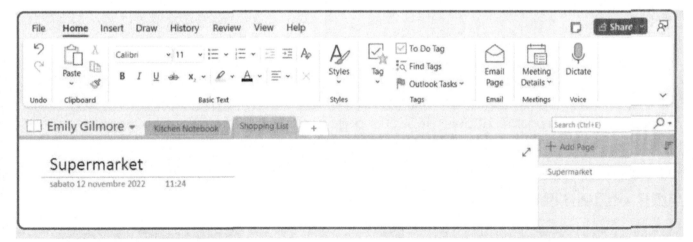

3. **Additional section options**:

- Right-clicking on a section tab also allows you to:
- Delete the section
- Export the section
- Create a **new section group**

4. **Creating a section group**:

This feature helps organize related sections together. For example, if you're expanding your notebook to cover all home-related information:

- Right-click on a section tab
- Select **"Create new section group"**
- A new group will appear above the canvas
- Rename the group by right-clicking on it

5. **Organizing sections within groups:**

- You can create different groups for various areas of your home
- Place relevant sections within each group
- For instance, you might have a **"Kitchen"** group containing sections like **"Recipes,"** **"Appliance Manuals,"** and **"Cleaning Tips"**

Home Tab

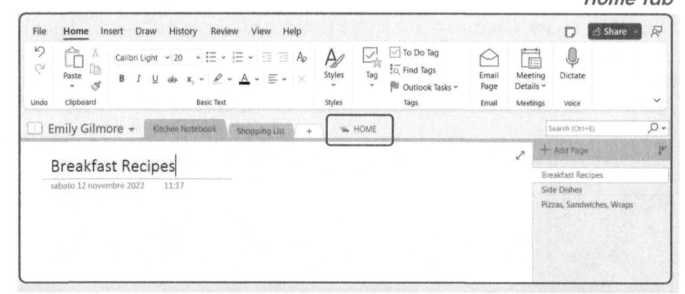

This hierarchical structure allows for better **organization** and easier **navigation** within your notebook, especially as it grows larger and more complex.

Using Templates and Other Formats

OneNote offers various ways to structure your pages. Let's explore these options:

1. **Using pre-made templates:**

- Navigate to the **insert tab** on the ribbon
- Click on **page templates** in the **pages** section
- Choose from various options like to-do lists, lecture notes, or index cards

- Once selected, your page will automatically update to the chosen template

Insert Tab

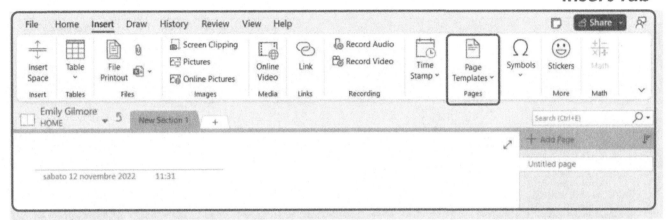

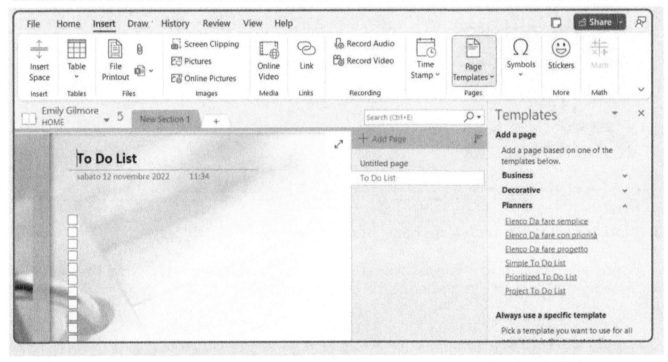

2. Custom formatting options:

If you prefer to customize your page yourself, OneNote provides several tools:

- **Spreadsheet**: Insert a mini Excel sheet directly into your note
- **Picture**: Add images to illustrate your notes
- **Video**: Embed video content for multimedia notes
- **Table**: Create organized data structures
- **Equations**: Insert mathematical formulas
- **Symbols**: Add special characters
- **Stickers**: Decorate your notes with fun graphics

All these options are available in the **insert tab** of the ribbon, grouped in relevant sections.

Insert Tab

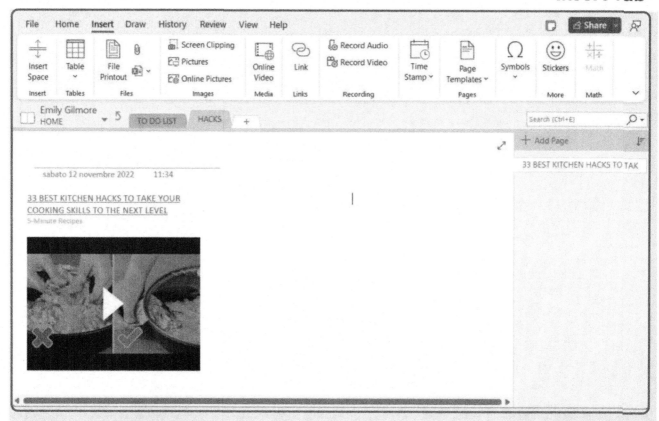

3. Working with inserted elements:

- Spreadsheets and tables are interactive; you can work directly within them
- Stickers are decorative and can't be edited once placed

Pro tip for working with images containing text: *OneNote has a powerful feature to extract text from images. Here's how to use it:*

1. *Copy and paste the image into your work area*
2. *Right-click on the image*
3. *Select* **copy text from picture**
4. *Click on another area of the canvas*
5. *The extracted text will appear, ready for you to edit as needed*

Page Settings

OneNote offers various options to customize your page layout. Let's explore these features:

1. **Page customization** (found in the view tab under page setup):

   - Change page color
   - Add rule lines (multiple styles available)
   - Hide page title
   - Switch to dark mode (via the **switch background** button)

View Tab

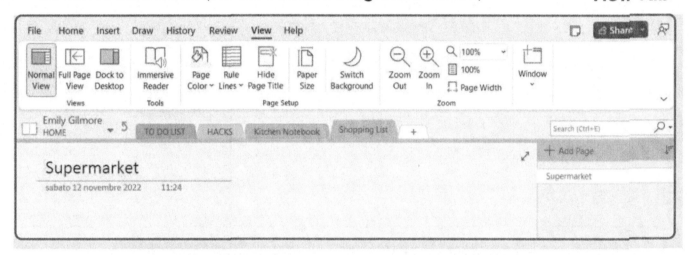

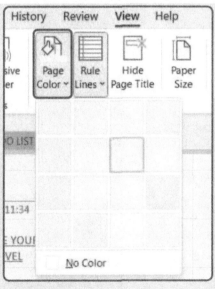

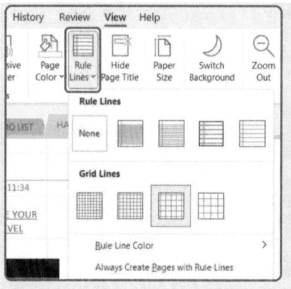

2. **Preparing for printing**: You can adjust the **paper format** to ensure your content fits within printable areas

   - Click on the **paper size** button
   - A pane will appear on the side of your window

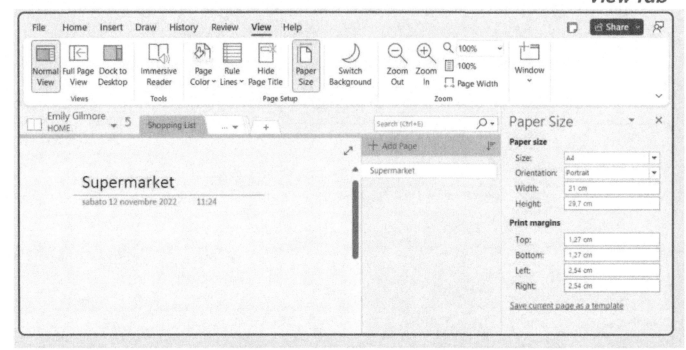

- Choose your options:
- Paper size
- Orientation (landscape or portrait)
- Margins

View Tab

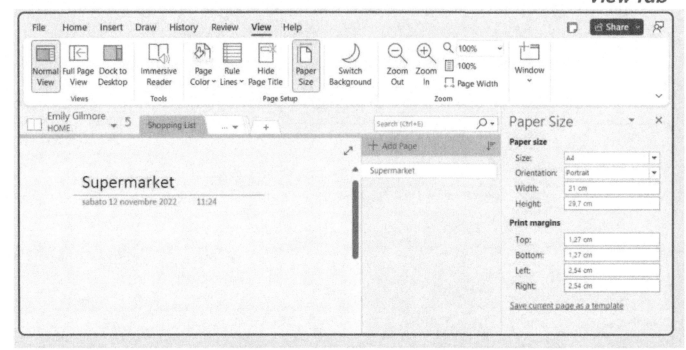

3. **Creating custom templates:** At the bottom of the paper size options, you'll find advanced settings:

- Check the box to save your settings as a template
- Name your template before saving
- Decide whether to apply this format to all pages in the section

Step-by-step guide to create a custom page format:

1. Go to the **view tab** on the ribbon
2. Locate the **page setup** section
3. Click on **paper size**
4. In the side pane, select your preferred:

- Paper size
- Orientation
- Margins

5. If you want to save as a template:

- Check the box at the bottom
- Give your template a name

6. Decide if you want to apply this format to all pages in the section
7. Click "Save" or "Apply" (depending on your choices)

Taking and Formatting Notes

After setting your page title, you're ready to start writing your notes. While plain text works fine, OneNote offers **tags** to make your document more user-friendly. You'll find these quick formatting options in the **home tab** of the ribbon, along with their **keyboard shortcuts** in parentheses. These tags include **to-do checkboxes**, icons for **passwords**, **addresses**, and **phone numbers**, as well as text **highlighting** options.

When you select a tag, it appears where your cursor was last positioned on the canvas. However, you can easily move tags around by **clicking and dragging** them to your preferred location. OneNote's free-form canvas allows you to place elements wherever you feel they fit best.

Selecting a tag brings up a box around it. Clicking the ellipsis at the top reveals more **quick options** for text formatting and modifications. You can also use the movement arrow to resize the dialogue box as needed. If you want to remove a tag you've created, you have two options: select it and press **delete**, or click the **X** button located in the **basic text section** of the **home tab**.

Home Tab

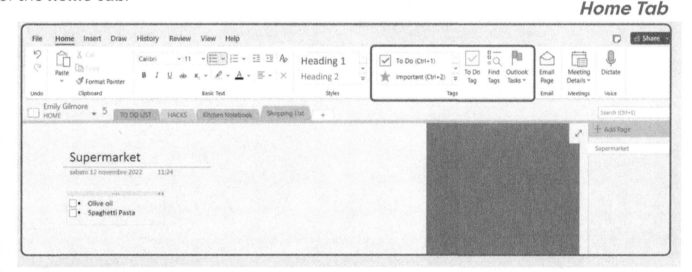

Searching for Tags

You can access this function by clicking the **find tags** button in the **tags section** of the home tab. This action opens a pane on your screen where you can search for tags by various criteria such as name, section, title, date, or note text. The search results will display a list of potential tags for you to choose from.

By default, OneNote searches for related tags throughout the entire notebook. However, you can modify this scope using options at the bottom of the **tags summary** pane. These options allow you to narrow your search to specific parts of your notebook, such as individual sections or pages. Additionally, you can filter tags based on their **creation time**, focusing on tags from the past week or even yesterday's notes.

OneNote also provides a handy feature to create an editable list of all your tags on a single notebook page. To use this feature, first select the page where you want to place the list.

Then, navigate to the tags summary pane and click the **create summary page** button. This action generates a comprehensive list of tags from your selected area and adds it to your chosen page. As with the search function, you can specify the time frame or location from which you want to pull the tags.

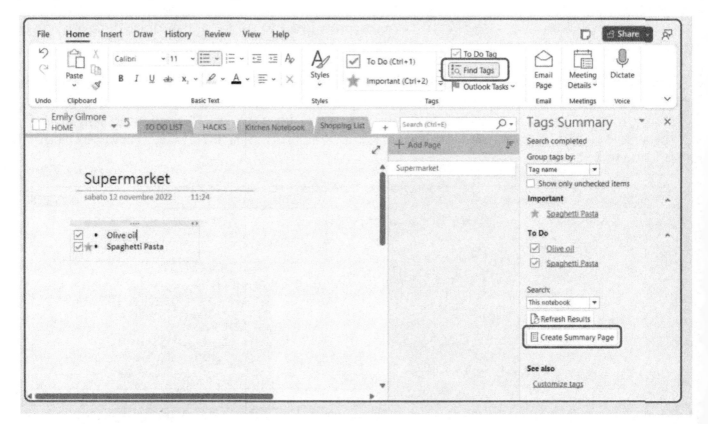

Customizing Tags

To create or modify tags in OneNote:

1. Go to the **home** pane
2. Click the **find tags** button
3. At the bottom of the pane, click **customize tags**

In the dialogue box that opens:

- Choose to create a new tag or modify an existing one
- For a new tag, click the **"New Tag"** button

When creating a new tag, set:

1. Name
2. Symbol (from available options)
3. Font color
4. Highlight option (on/off)

A preview window shows how your tag will look. Click **ok** to create your new tag.

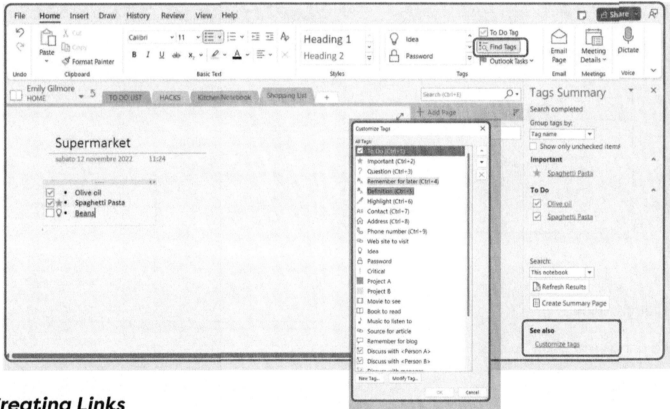

Creating Links

The ability to link from one section to another is one of OneNote's best features. The **create links section** that appears when you click the right mouse button makes this possible.

Steps to create a link:

1. Select the place in the canvas for the link
2. Right-click and choose **link**
3. In the dialogue box, type the display text

Link options:

1. Link to external content:

- Choose a document on your device
- Add a webpage URL

2. Link to internal OneNote content:

- **Browse** through available notebooks and sections
- Select a page or section to link
- Click **ok** to create the link

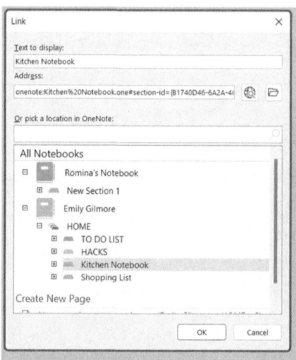

After creating:

Use **drag and drop** to position the link where needed

Benefits:

- Easily navigate between related information

  - Improves efficiency when working with complex or extensive notes

  - Helps maintain context when dealing with interconnected ideas

- Connect ideas across different notebooks

  - Ideal for projects that span multiple areas or subjects
  - Facilitates a more holistic approach to note-taking and information management

- Integrate external resources into your notes

  - Enhances the depth and breadth of your notes
  - Keeps all relevant information centralized within OneNote

Drawing and Sketching in OneNote

OneNote offers a robust set of **drawing and sketching features**, particularly beneficial for users with **mobile devices** like tablets. These tools are conveniently located in the **draw tab** of the ribbon, providing a range of options to enhance your note-taking experience.

The **drawing tools** allow for **freehand drawing** directly on the canvas, which is especially useful if you're using a **stylus** with your tablet. To start drawing, simply select a **pen tool** from the draw tab and begin creating on the canvas. It's worth experimenting with different pen types, such as ballpoint or felt tip, to achieve various effects in your notes.

Draw Tab

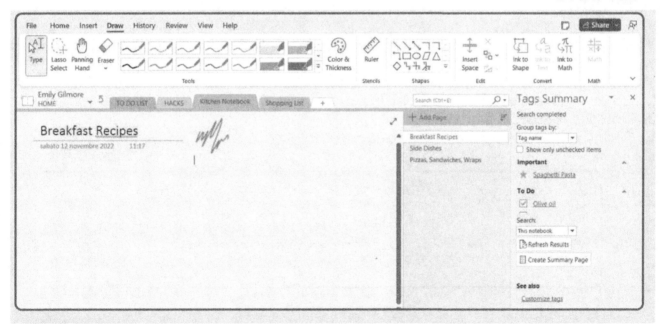

In addition to freehand drawing, OneNote provides **pre-made shapes** in the **shapes section**. You can easily insert these by clicking on the desired shape and then clicking and dragging on the canvas to create it. If you prefer, you can also draw shapes manually using the freehand drawing tool.

Customization is a key feature of OneNote's drawing tools. You can adjust the **thickness** of lines, choose different **colors**, and even add **highlighting** effects. To customize your drawing tool, select it and then use the options in the draw tab to make your adjustments. Creating a custom color palette can be helpful for maintaining consistent styling across your notes.

For corrections, OneNote includes an **eraser tool** with adjustable size for precision. To use it, click on the eraser tool, adjust its size if needed, and then click and drag over the area you want to erase. Using a smaller eraser size can be particularly useful for detailed corrections.

OneNote also offers impressive **conversion features** for hand-drawn content. The "**Ink to Shape**" option can transform rough sketches into precise geometric shapes, which is great for creating diagrams or flowcharts. "**Ink to Text**" converts handwritten notes into typed text, perfect for digitizing meeting notes or ideas. For those working with mathematical content, "**Ink to Math**" can convert handwritten equations into properly formatted digital equations.

To use these conversion features, start by drawing or writing on the canvas with your preferred tool. Then select the appropriate conversion option from the Draw tab. A new window will open where you can recreate your original drawing or writing. OneNote will automatically convert your input to digital format in real-time.

Recording

OneNote enables users to **record audio and video** directly within the app. These recordings become part of your notebook. To access this feature:

1. Go to the **Insert tab** in the ribbon
2. Find the **Recording option**
3. Choose between **audio** or **video recording**

Insert Tab

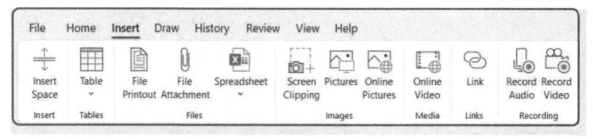

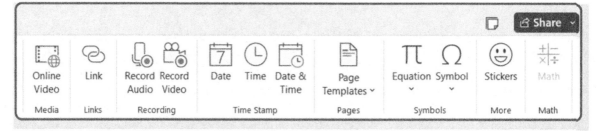

When you click **Record Audio**, a thumbnail labeled **Audio Recording** appears on your canvas. However, this doesn't mean the recording is complete - it's just begun! The device continues recording until you hit the **pause or stop button** in the ribbon. Remember this unique feature, as it's uncommon to see the icon before finishing the process.

After creating an audio or video file, a new **Playback tab** appears above the status bar in the ribbon. This taskbar is specifically for managing audio and video recordings in OneNote. Here, you can **play or forward** media, adjust playback, and access **settings**.

Playback Tab

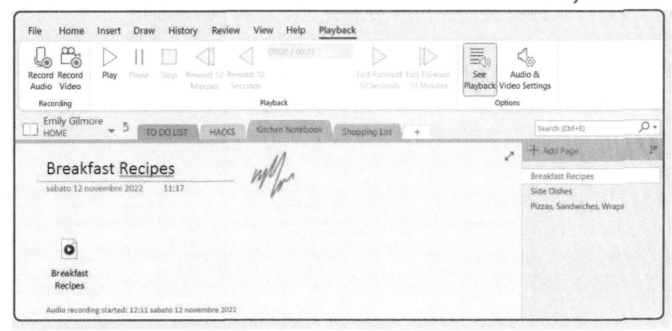

The settings menu is identical to the one in the Options menu under the File tab, but it takes you directly to the device's audio and video settings. Ensure your **microphone and camera are enabled** for optimal recording quality.

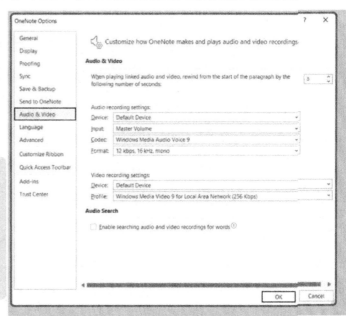

> ***Pro tip:*** *When first opening OneNote, the page and section pane is typically on the right side of your canvas. If you prefer it on the left, go to the **Display option** in the OneNote Options menu and select **Move Page List to the Left** for a more comfortable workflow.*

Sharing and Synchronizing

OneNote can communicate with other programs in the Microsoft Suite, particularly Outlook, which is the last thing you need to know about it. This integration offers several powerful features:

1. **Task Synchronization:** You can create tasks in OneNote that automatically sync with Outlook

   - Click the **Outlook Tasks** button in the **Tags** section of the ribbon.
   - Choose when you want the task completed. (You can see the keyboard shortcuts for doing so, too).
   - Write the task description on the canvas
   - The task will appear in Outlook with a link to the OneNote page

Home Tab

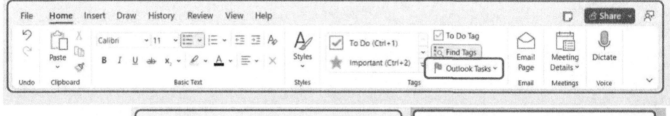

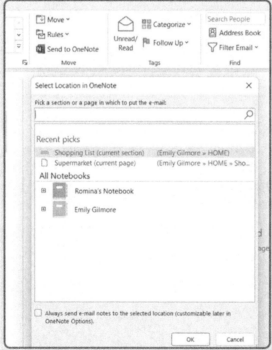

Send Task on Outlook to One Note

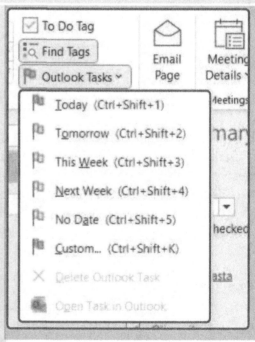

Pro Tip: *This synchronization works both ways. In Outlook, use the **OneNote** button to create tasks that appear in OneNote.*

2. **Email Notebook Pages:** Share individual notebook pages without exposing your entire notebook

- Go to the **Home tab** in the ribbon
- Click the **Email Page** button
- An email will open with the page content in the body
- Add recipients and use Outlook features as needed

3. **Password Protection:** Secure sensitive information in your notebook:

- Go to the **Review** tab
- Click the yellow **Password** padlock
- Set a password in the protection pane

Review Tab

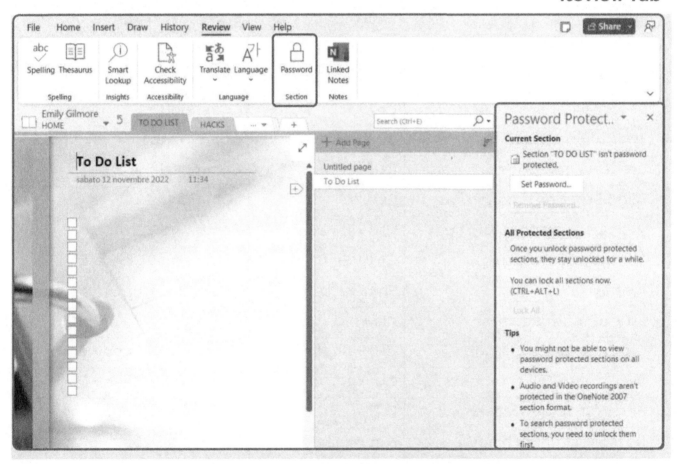

Note: Password-protected sections can't be searched unless unlocked.

4. **Meeting Synchronization:** OneNote automatically syncs with your Outlook calendar:

- Click **Meeting Details** in the **Meetings section** of the **Home tab**
- View today's meetings or search for future ones
- Select a meeting to open a note-taking page

- Take notes and easily email them to all participants

When you click the button, it will either display the meetings you have scheduled for that day or give you the option to look up other meetings. After choosing the meeting you want to record notes for, click on it to bring up a dialogue box where you can add information.

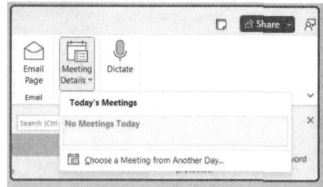

Keyboard Shortcuts on OneNote

Function	Shortcut on PC	Shortcut on Mac
Create a link	Ctrl + K	Command + K
Search all notebooks	Ctrl + E	Command + E
Search the current page	Ctrl + F	Command + F
Type a math equation	Alt + +	Not available
Create a new page	Ctrl + N	Command + N
Align paragraph to the left	Ctrl + L	Command + L
Align paragraph to the right	Ctrl + R	Command + R
Show or hide line rules	Ctrl + Shift + R	Command + Shift + R
Insert a line break	Shift + Enter	Option + Return
Start a math equation	Alt + =	Control + =
Close current notebook	Ctrl + Shift + W	Command + Shift + W
Synchronize all notebooks	Ctrl + S	Command + Shift + S
Enter full screen mode	F11	Command + Control + F
Review list of open notebooks	Not available	Control + G
Open other notebooks	Ctrl + O	Command + O
Switch between sections	Ctrl + Tab	Command + Shift + { or }
Insert emoji	Alt + N, S	Command + Control + Space
Insert current date	Alt + Shift + D	Command + D

Chapter 10:
Microsoft Publisher

Enhancing Layout and Design

While Microsoft Word excels at document creation and text editing, **Publisher fills a crucial gap by offering advanced page layout capabilities**. Publisher was developed to help users design invitations, business letters, and cards with precise formatting. It serves as a cost-effective alternative to more expensive software with similar functions.

With Publisher, you can create magazine layouts and format documents to match your vision. This tool empowers users to configure pages exactly as they envision them, going beyond Word's capabilities. In this chapter, we'll explore how to leverage Publisher's features to achieve your desired document layouts and designs. Let's dive into the process of creating professionally formatted documents using this versatile software.

Setting Up the Page

When you open a new document, you'll see **blue margins** that define your working area. Unlike Word, Publisher requires you to use the **Margins button** in the **Page Design** tab to

adjust these margins. This tab also allows you to change the **page orientation** and **paper size**.

To enhance your layout process, Publisher provides **grid lines** and **guides**. These tools are especially useful when creating documents like flyers or magazine-style layouts. The **Guides button** in the **Layout** section of the Page Design tab offers various options for setting up your page structure. These guidelines and margin lines are visible only during the design process and won't appear in the final printed document.

HomeTab

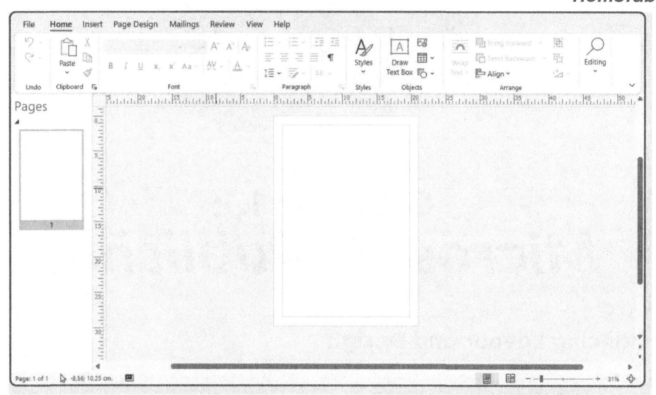

Setting Up Basic Page Layout:

1. Open a new document in Publisher
2. Navigate to the **Page Design** tab in the ribbon
3. Use the **Margins** button to adjust page margins
4. Set **Orientation** (portrait or landscape) as needed
5. Choose the appropriate **Paper Size** for your project

Using Grid Lines and Guides:

1. In the Page Design tab, find the **Layout** section
2. Click on the **Guides** button
3. Select the type of guides you want to use
4. Adjust the guides to fit your layout needs

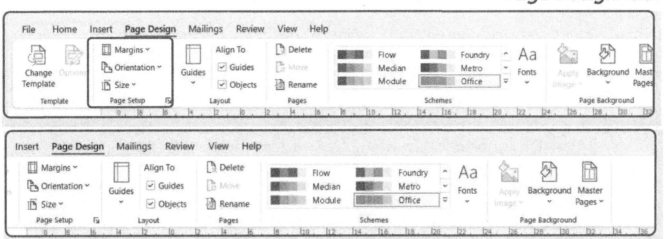

After setting up your grid lines, you'll notice they've been placed on your document. These lines are flexible and can be easily adjusted to suit your layout needs. To reposition a grid line, simply click on it and use the drag-and-drop method to move it to your desired location.

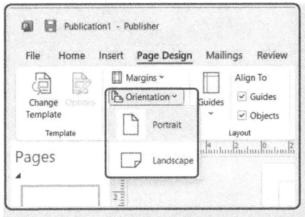

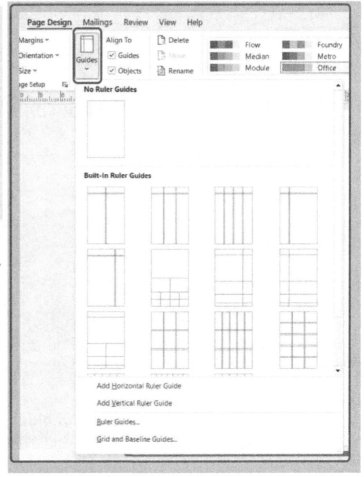

There's no limit to the number of grid lines you can add, allowing you to create a highly customized format for your document. If you find you've added a grid line by mistake or no longer need one, removing it is just as simple. Click on the unwanted line and drag it beyond the page boundaries - this action will delete it from your file.

This intuitive system of adding, moving, and removing grid lines gives you complete control over your document's structure, enabling you to create precisely the layout you envision.

Inserting Elements to Your File

Before you start creating content, it's crucial to set up your page correctly. To begin adding text to your document, locate the **draw text box** button in the home tab of the ribbon. This tool allows you to add text elements to your layout.

Upon selecting this option, you'll have the flexibility to determine the size of your text box. It's important to remember that for proper saving and printing later on, this text box must be positioned within the established grid and margin lines. This careful placement ensures that your content will appear as intended in the final document.

After designating the area for your text, simply release the mouse button, and you'll see that the box automatically adjusts to fit within the page parameters. At this point, you're ready to start inputting your content.

Text Box Tab

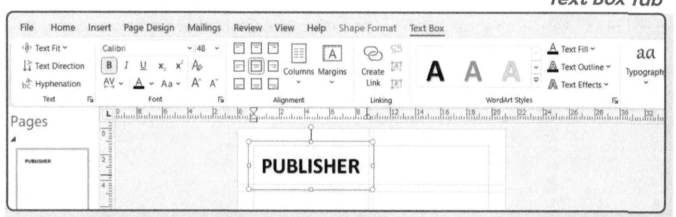

To explore additional elements for your publication, navigate to the **insert tab** on the ribbon. This section offers a variety of standard features to enhance your document:

- Calendars
- Bookmarks for specific pages
- Headers and footers
- Custom page borders
- Picture placeholders

Publisher provides flexibility in terms of image insertion. You can incorporate images from online sources or your local computer.

If you haven't yet selected the specific image you want to use, Publisher offers a convenient solution. You can insert a **picture placeholder** as a temporary stand-in. This allows you to continue designing your layout without interrupting your workflow, and you can easily replace the placeholder with your chosen image later.

Insert Tab

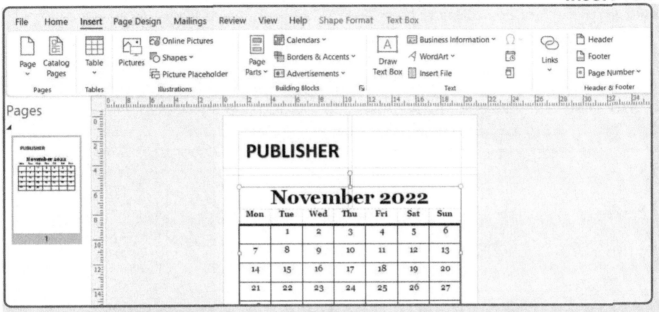

Pro tip: *The majority of the features that Publisher allows you to add are editable. This means that even though it gives you a specific format, you can modify it to suit your preferences and style it with, for instance, the colors of your company or school by clicking the right button on top of these elements.*

Familiar Tools

Microsoft Publisher shares many familiar features with other Microsoft Office applications, particularly in its **text formatting capabilities**. The **home tab** houses a suite of text formatting tools that mirror those found in programs like Word, allowing users to customize their text appearance with ease.

Home Tab

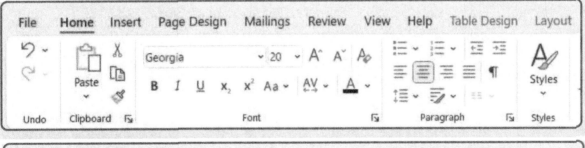

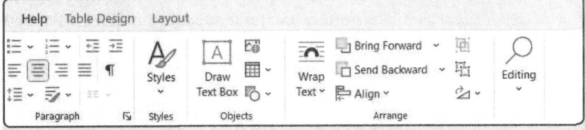

This familiarity extends to the document overview, where Publisher employs a **thumbnail view** reminiscent of PowerPoint, providing a comprehensive visual representation of your publication's structure.

Adding pages in Publisher is a straightforward process, achievable through multiple methods. Users can **right-click on the thumbnail pane** and select **"add page,"** or navigate to the **insert tab** and utilize the **page button** in the pages section.

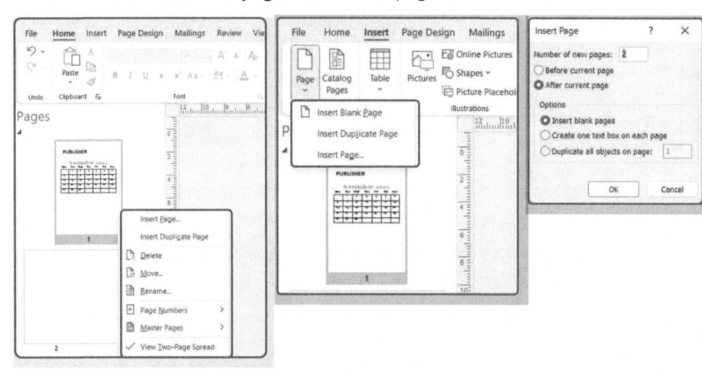

Publisher distinguishes itself by offering a **double-page view** option, catering to projects that require a spread layout, such as booklets or magazines.

View Tab

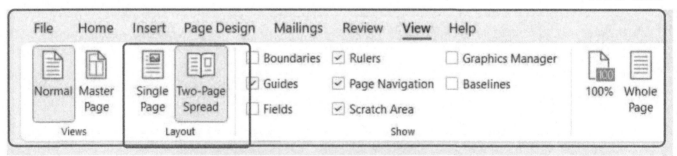

The software's flexibility shines in its **page management capabilities**. Users can effortlessly reorder pages by dragging thumbnails or using the **move button** in the **page design tab**. This tab also houses options to **rename** or **delete** pages, providing comprehensive control over the document's structure. When adding new pages, it's important to note that while margins carry over from the initial setup, **guides** need to be reinserted manually.

Page Design Tab

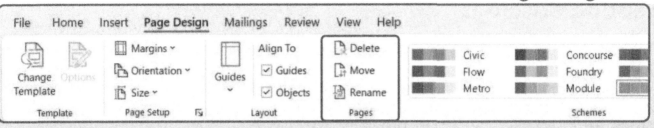

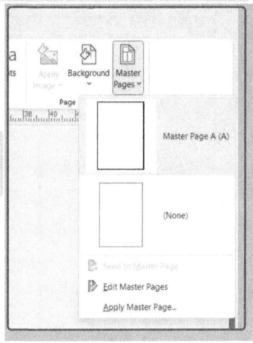

Pro tip: *Go to the* **view tab** *on the ribbon and select the* **single page or two-page spread buttons** *to see a single page or a double page view.*

Publisher's **master page** feature, accessible via the page design tab, allows for consistent formatting across your document. By customizing the master page, users can establish a standardized layout that automatically applies to new pages, ensuring visual coherence throughout the publication.

The software incorporates a range of familiar elements from other Office applications, including **tables**, **WordArt**, **headers and footers**, and **page numbers**. The process for inserting images and files mirrors that of other Microsoft programs, maintaining a consistent user experience across the Office suite. Additionally, Publisher includes essential tools like **spell check** and **translation functions** in multiple languages, further enhancing its utility as a comprehensive publishing tool.

Insert Tab

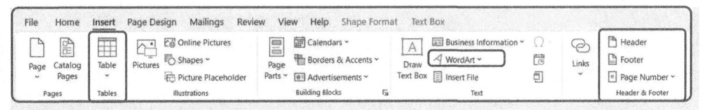

Creating Catalogs

Publisher offers a specialized tool for **business owners** looking to create product **catalogs**. This feature streamlines the process of showcasing your offerings in a professional format. To begin, navigate to the **insert tab** on the ribbon and select the **catalog pages** button. This action not only inserts a pre-formatted catalog page but also activates an additional **catalog format** tab in the ribbon, providing specific tools for catalog design.

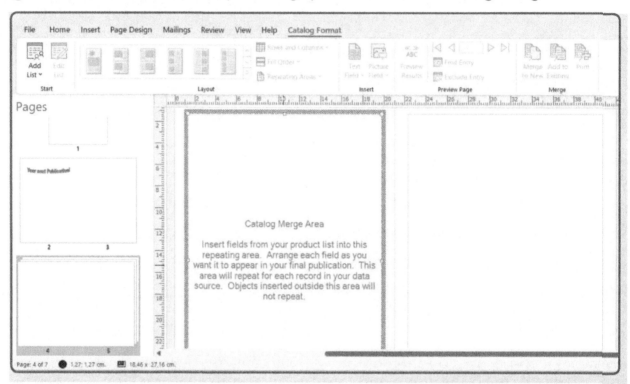

The catalog format allows you to organize your products in **boxes**, creating a **user-friendly layout**. Within the **layout area**, you can customize the design to accommodate your specific needs, adjusting the space allocation for each product based on your inventory size.

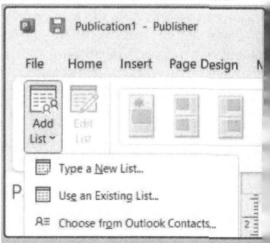

To enhance organization and tracking, Publisher enables the creation of a product **list**. Access this feature through the **add list** button in the catalog format tab.

Create a Product List

- Click the **Add List** button in the **Catalog Format tab**
- In the dialog box, add entries for each product:

- Product name
- Description
- ID number
- Price
- Picture (if available)

- Use the **Add**, **Delete**, and **Customize** options as needed

Once you've compiled your product information, Publisher automatically generates a savable list. This feature proves particularly useful for future catalog updates or creating new product showcases, as it allows you to easily **reuse and modify** your existing product database.

> **Pro tip:** You will be able to add products to the dialogue boxes you create for the catalog in accordance with the built-in product list once you have done so. The data box containing the pertinent information you want to include will be made up of the list you created. Go to the **edit list button** on the ribbon to make the necessary adjustments if the list needs to be modified to better suit your file.

If you're making a catalog of items that are on sale, Publisher may be all you need to use to add specific stickers. Look for the **advertisements button** under **the insert tab** on the ribbon. When you click on it, a number of sticker options that can be used in your file for sales and other events will appear.

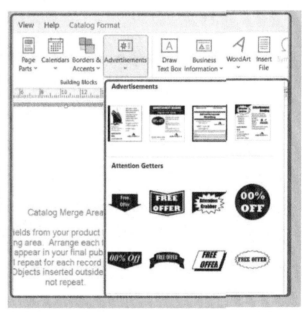

These stickers offer quick access to highlighting a product, though you can still search the internet for other fashionable options. Additionally, by clicking on the image with the right button and customizing it to your liking, you can change its color, font, and style.

Creating Mailing Lists

One of Publisher's key advantages is its robust **mailing system** capabilities. The **mail merge tool** allows you to incorporate mailing addresses into your publications or personalize content for individual recipients. For instance, you can use client names from a list to customize each document. This process begins by selecting your data source: an existing **Excel spreadsheet**, an **Access database**, your **Outlook contacts**, or a newly created list.

After choosing your data source, you'll specify where in the document to insert the personalized information. The result is a set of **customized documents**, each tailored to a specific recipient. If you find this process challenging, Publisher offers a **mail merge wizard** that provides step-by-step guidance.

Publisher also supports **email merges**, following a similar process but using email addresses instead of physical ones. Upon completion, the program seamlessly integrates with Outlook to facilitate sending. Like its mail counterpart, this feature includes a **wizard** for user assistance.

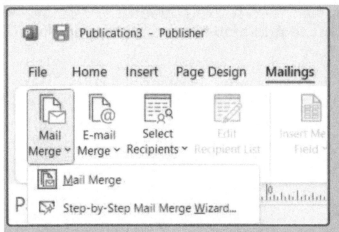
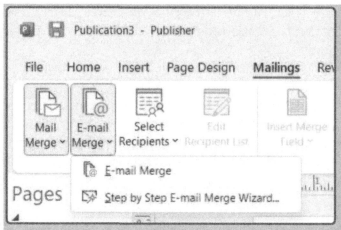

For those without an existing contact list, Publisher allows you to **create a new recipient list** on the spot.

Access this feature through the **Select Recipients** button in the **Mailings tab**, choosing the **Type a New List** option. You can later modify this list using the **Edit Recipient List** button.

These **mailing tools** significantly enhance Publisher's utility, enabling users to create personalized, professional-looking communications efficiently.

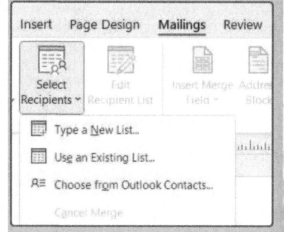

Streamlining Business Document Creation in Publisher

Publisher offers a convenient way to **manage and incorporate business information** into your documents. This feature is particularly useful for maintaining consistency across various publications and saving time on repetitive data entry.

To set up your business details:

1. Click on the **File tab** in the ribbon
2. Select the **Info** button
3. Choose **Edit Business Information**
4. A dialog box will appear where you can input relevant details
5. You can even add a **company logo** for a professional touch
6. After entering the information, click **Save** to store it

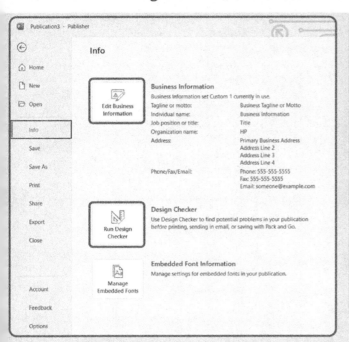

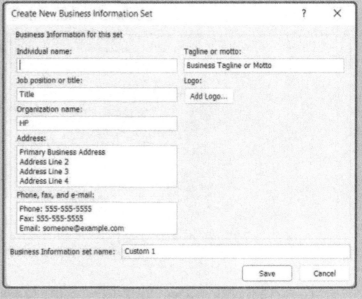

Once saved, this business information becomes readily accessible throughout Publisher. You can quickly insert these details into any document by:

1. Navigating to the **Insert tab** on the ribbon
2. Clicking on the **Business Information** button
3. Selecting the desired information from the dropdown menu

This **streamlined process** ensures that your business details are always up-to-date and easily insertable into any publication. It's especially helpful for creating professional-looking documents such as letterheads, business cards, or promotional materials.

Pro tip: *The Business Information section also allows for quick edits. If you need to update any details, you can do so directly from the dropdown menu in the Insert tab, ensuring your information stays current across all your Publisher documents.*

Design Checker

The **Design Checker** is a crucial feature in Publisher that helps ensure your documents are free from common design errors before printing or saving. This tool is accessible through the **Info section** of the **File tab** in the ribbon.

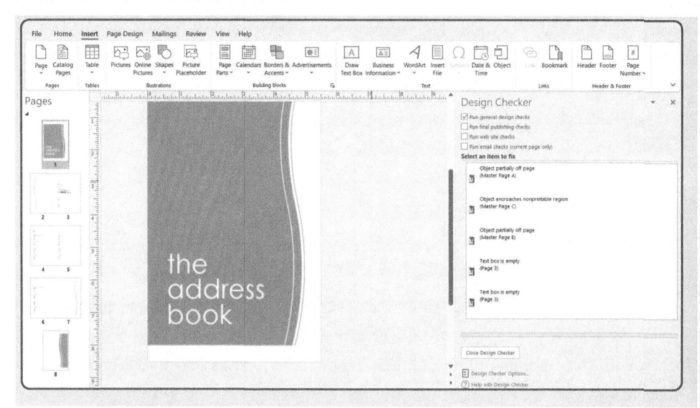

To use the Design Checker:

1. Click on the **File tab**
2. Select **Info**
3. Click the **Design Check button**

This action returns you to your working canvas and opens a pane on the right side of the window. Here, you can select from various check options:

- General design checks
- Publishing checks
- Website checks
- Email checks (for the current page only)

As you select each check type, the **errors automatically update** in the dialog box below. This box displays issues that need addressing within your project, such as:

- Items outside the page boundaries
- White spaces on the page
- Text overflowing margins

Each error is linked to its specific page location, allowing for easy identification and correction.

To fine-tune the Design Checker:

1. Scroll to the bottom of the dialog box
2. Click on **Design Checker Options**
3. In the new dialog box, you can:

- Choose how errors are sorted
- Set the page range for checking
- Specify which types of errors to highlight

After adjusting these settings, you can run the Design Checker again for a more tailored review.

This feature is invaluable for **maintaining professional standards** in your publications. By catching and correcting design errors before finalizing your document, you ensure a polished, error-free final product.

Whether you're creating business materials, websites, or email campaigns, the Design Checker helps maintain the quality and professionalism of your Publisher projects.

Keyboard Shortcuts on Publisher

Function	Shortcut on PC	Shortcut on Mac
New Publication	Ctrl + N	Command + N
Open Publication	Ctrl + O	Command + O
Save	Ctrl + S	Command + S
Print	Ctrl + P	Command + P
Undo	Ctrl + Z	Command + Z
Redo	Ctrl + Y	Command + Y
Cut	Ctrl + X	Command + X

Keyboard Shortcuts on Publisher

Function	Shortcut on PC	Shortcut on Mac
Copy	Ctrl + C	Command + C
Paste	Ctrl + V	Command + V
Select All	Ctrl + A	Command + A
Find	Ctrl + F	Command + F
Replace	Ctrl + H	Command + H
Bold	Ctrl + B	Command + B
Italic	Ctrl + I	Command + I
Underline	Ctrl + U	Command + U
Align Left	Ctrl + L	Command + L
Align Center	Ctrl + E	Command + E
Align Right	Ctrl + R	Command + R
Justify	Ctrl + J	Command + J
Increase Font Size	Ctrl + Shift + >	Command + Shift + >
Decrease Font Size	Ctrl + Shift + <	Command + Shift + <
Zoom In	Ctrl + +	Command + +
Zoom Out	Ctrl + -	Command + -
Insert Page	Ctrl + Shift + N	Command + Shift + N
Show/Hide Rulers	Alt + Shift + R	Option + Shift + R
Group Objects	Ctrl + G	Command + G
Ungroup Objects	Ctrl + Shift + G	Command + Shift + G
Bring to Front	Ctrl + Shift + F	Command + Shift + F
Send to Back	Ctrl + Shift + B	Command + Shift + B

Note: Some of these shortcuts may vary depending on the version of Microsoft Publisher you're using. Also, Publisher for Mac might not have all the features available in the Windows version, so some shortcuts may not be applicable.

Conclusion

This tutorial has provided a comprehensive understanding of the Microsoft Office suite. **Readers have learned essential skills for creating documents in Word, managing data in Excel, designing presentations in PowerPoint, and handling emails in Outlook.** These four core applications are crucial for anyone looking to enhance their software proficiency, especially in a corporate environment.

The tutorial went beyond these basics, covering database creation in Access, communication via Skype and Teams, secure file storage with OneDrive, survey creation in Forms, note-taking in OneNote, and layout design in Publisher. **Congratulations on mastering these tools!** It's worth noting that many software applications share similar layouts and icons, making it easier to navigate between them. The ribbon interface, common across most applications, can significantly boost productivity when used effectively.

This book aims to serve as a comprehensive guide, addressing any uncertainties about these programs. Each section includes keyboard shortcuts, many of which are consistent across applications, like the universal copy and paste commands (Ctrl + C and Ctrl + V). These shortcuts can help optimize your workflow and save time when creating files.

Keep this book as a reference, readily available whenever you need to refresh your memory or clarify a concept. If you need to revisit any section, don't hesitate to reread the relevant chapter. Most of the information should remain applicable despite potential software updates.

Users should feel confident using this software, and the knowledge gained is expected to be valuable in both personal and professional settings. **If readers have found this book helpful in improving their understanding of program management in daily life, we encourage them to share their thoughts by leaving a review and comment.** Your feedback is valuable and will help improve future content.

Best of luck in your future endeavors!

GET YOUR FREE BOOK BONUSES NOW!

(DOWNLOAD FOR FREE WITH THE BELOW INSTRUCTION!)

DO YOU WANT TO UNLOCK THE FULL KNOWLEDGE ABOUT MICROSOFT OFFICE SUITE?

1) BONUS 1: 300+ Excel Templates: Business | Personal | Project | Tracker | Chart | Invoice | List | Calendar | Analysis | Schedule | Budget

2) BONUS 2: Guide on How to Manage your Time

3) BONUS 3: Guide on How to Manage your Productivity

4) BONUS 4: Guide on How to Prepare Yourself For a Job Interview

5) BONUS 5: How to Improve Fast your Office 365 Skills

SCAN THE QR CODE BELOW AND UNLOCK THE FULL POTENTIAL OF OFFICE 365 SUITE!!

SCAN ME

INDEX

INDEX

S

Printed in Great Britain
by Amazon